CLASSICAL
MUSIC

CLASSICAL MUSIC

An Informal Guide

RICHARD CARLIN

a cappella books

Library of Congress Cataloging-in-Publication Data

Carlin, Richard.
    Classical music : an informal guide / Richard Carlin.
        p. cm.
    Includes index.
    ISBN 1-55652-148-0 : $11.95
    1. Music appreciation. 2. Compact discs—Reviews. I. Title.
MT90.C372   1992
781.6'8—dc20   92-1176
                                                        CIP
                                                        MN

Published by
a cappella books, incorporated
an imprint of Chicago Review Press

Printed in the United States of America
5 4 3 2 1

Editorial offices:
P.O. Box 380
Pennington, New Jersey 08534

Business/sales offices:
814 North Franklin Street
Chicago, Illinois 60610

Cover art: *Intermission* by George Schreiber, 1954. Lithograph published by Associated American Artists. From the collection of Minerva Fruchtbaum. Used by permission.

To Jessica

CONTENTS

ACKNOWLEDGMENTS

Thanks to Curt Matthews for suggesting that I write this book, and for making this and all other a cappella books possible. To Linda Matthews for a keen and wise editorial eye; Susan Bindig for careful and thorough fact-checking and copyediting; Amy Teschner for editorial input; Mark Suchomel for playing the accordion and helping to sell the book; Ellen Dessloch for my worldwide author's tour; Michelle Barliant for able representation to music stores; Lee Swets for getting this from disc to page; Cynthia Gordon for paying the bills; Fran Lee for a beautiful cover; and all the rest of the staff at Chicago Review Press. To the Musical Heritage Society for supporting my career as a classical music critic, and to James Warren for editorial guidance in the past. To my brother, whose musical tastes range from Blind Lemon Jefferson to Moby Grape, to my parents, for piano lessons and taking me to the Young People's concerts, and to Jessica, without whom there would be no music at all.

ONE
ENJOYING
CLASSICAL MUSIC

Classical Music: An Informal Guide is a beginner's guide to classical or art music created over the last 500 years. It features the instrumental music of three periods: the Baroque, Classical, and Romantic eras (see chapter 2). This is the time, from about 1650–1900, when the best-known classical music was created. We will be focusing on the greatest composers and their most famous compositions, giving some background for their achievements so that you can better enjoy their music.

Our goal is "enjoyment;" after all, we listen to music for pleasure, not to have a "cultural experience." Classical music can be fun, and it doesn't take a lot of effort or education to learn to appreciate it. With this in mind, we've tried not to take our task too seriously. We'll enjoy our journey by taking some side trips and detours as well as following the beaten path.

After some introductory material defining the terrain and introducing classical-music styles and the musical instruments, the book proceeds chronologically, giving background on each era and then listing key composers with their compositions. There's also a handy timeline in Appendix B to help you along. Occasionally, we'll break the flow with a list of related music, some interesting facts, pop quizzes, and trivial pursuits to make reading a little more fun. And although this is not a comprehensive listener's guide, we will give an annotated list of many key recordings available on CD. After all, you want to *listen* to this music, not just read about it.

I am not a classical-music scholar, nor do I pretend to be one. However, I have extensive background writing about this music, and I'm an avid and enthusiastic listener. I won't be offering you breathtaking analyses of individual pieces of music; nor will I try to impress you with my erudition. Rather, I hope to act as a benevolent tour guide, sometimes following my own agenda, sometimes bowing to your needs. The point of this book is to inspire your own explorations, and if I can point out a few monuments along the way, I hope you will take the initiative to revisit them on your own. For this reason, a bibliography of sensible books is included, many of which influenced my own thinking and hopefully will inspire yours.

Common Fallacies and Fears
of the Beginning Listener

Beginning listeners to classical music often start with a favorite composition, instrument, or composer. But then they encounter various "traps" when they try to build on what they already enjoy. One listener said to me, "I love 'The Four Seasons' by Vivaldi and want to try something similar. A friend recommended that I buy the Brandenburg Concerti by Bach. When I got the CD home, it wasn't anything like the Vivaldi. How come?"

This is the "all-concerti-are-the-same" fallacy. Two different composers can write in a particular form, such as the concerto, and come up with quite different results. They live at different times, in different countries, and have different artistic goals. If you enjoy Vivaldi, you might explore other Italian composers for the violin.

Another common upset is the "all-works-by-one-composer-are-the-same" trap: "I like Bach's violin sonatas, so I bought a CD of his organ works. But, where the violin works were light and airy, the organ works were ponderous and dull and gave me a headache. Now I'm not sure I like Bach at all!"

Bach was a journeyman composer, working at the whim of his different employers at different stages of his life. So, his religious music is quite different from his secular music; works written in youth can be very different from mature works; works written for instructional purposes differ from those written to celebrate a specific event. Nobody likes everything Bach wrote (probably not even Mrs. Bach), so you have to explore to find what appeals to you most.

Sometimes a poor recording or performance can turn you off to a great piece of music. The Podunk Symphony may not have the technical expertise to tackle Beethoven's ninth symphony. Be sure that you're hearing a top-notch performance before you make a bottom-line judgment.

Experiencing Classical Music

If you are lucky enough to live in a major metropolitan area, you have the opportunity to hear classical music in concert. But attending a classical concert can be a daunting experience: you are expected to dress differently than in your everyday clothes, applaud only at the appropriate moment, cough (politely) only when there is a gap in the music, and sit quietly in your seat throughout the program. The musicians dress formally, rarely if ever speak directly to the audience, and often fail to acknowledge its presence at all. Ticket prices are high, and the general atmosphere discourages the attendance of the young or the uninitiated. To make matters more difficult, you have to plan ahead to attend a concert, purchasing tickets, arranging for baby-sitters, and generally working up enough energy to get to the concert hall.

Most of us experience classical music through recordings or radio. Yet, the number of commercial radio stations playing classical music has dwindled to a handful, and even public radio stations have begun to abandon the format in favor of all-talk or news. A recent survey showed that classical stations attracted only 1.7 percent of all listeners, falling behind religious broadcasters and, of course, coming way behind Top 40 or album-oriented radio. With the cutthroat commercial atmosphere in radio, this means that new commercial classical stations are unlikely to open.

Buying a classical-music recording is also off-putting for most beginning consumers. If you're looking for, say, "The Four Seasons" by Vivaldi, you're likely to find more than one option: budget-priced recordings, recordings by "big name" orchestras or conductors, recordings on "original instruments," recordings by foreign and domestic orchestras. The latest *Schwann* catalog, the record industry's most comprehensive guide to in-print recordings, lists no less than eighty-four different releases for this one work! Faced with these choices, consumers often go for the "pretty cover" approach ("I take the one that looks nicest"), or the "big name" approach ("I've heard of Leonard Bernstein . . ."), or the "cheapskate" approach ("Gee, $1.99 for a CD is a real bargain!").

All of these approaches are legitimate, as long as you know what you're getting. A budget-priced CD, for example, is likely to be an older recording poorly transferred to digital format (in other words, the sound quality will leave something to be desired). Some budget releases are re-issues of earlier recordings that were originally sold at a higher price. Most of the major labels have budget series, such as Columbia's Odyssey or RCA's Silver Seal, that offer good buys on very fine older recordings. Paying for a big name usually ensures a good performance, although Leonard Bernstein was a better interpreter of the Romantics than of Vivaldi, for example. And buying a record because it looks nice is great if you plan to leave it on your coffee table.

Record companies have thought of all kinds of ways to package classical music to entice the beginning listener. I'll assume that you are smart enough to avoid the "101 Classical Themes" collections, but you might be attracted by Columbia's *Classical Jukebox* ("all-time favorites by Bach, Brahms, Copland, Tchaikovsky, Rossini, more"; Columbia Masterworks MDK 45737) or *Mozart Goes to a Party* (What did he wear?; Columbia Masterworks MDK 46267). Actually, these collections often feature perfectly legitimate recordings by well-known artists. Still, there's something vaguely embarrassing about asking your record store for *Vivaldi's Greatest Hits* (spin another platter, Antonio!). In one of the more unusual marriages of art and commerce, Columbia Masterworks contracted good-housekeeping guru Martha Stewart to package several CDs entitled *Dinner Classics*, ranging from *Breakfast in Bed* (MFK 46356) to *A Cocktail Party* (MFK 46357), *Sunday Brunch* (two CDs: MFK 45547 and 46359), and *Dinner for Two* (MFK 46355). Each CD is an anthology of various classical works chosen to create the perfect mood for everything from Cheerios to Chivas Regal.

A major problem facing the beginning buyer is simply finding classical recordings. If you live in a major metropolitan area, you can probably find a store that offers a full stock of major composers; some will offer more than one recording of single works. However, if you live anywhere outside of a big city, you will be faced with scanty if any selection. Record clubs offer the option of buying through the mail; currently there are three classical record clubs, two operated by the major labels (Columbia House operated by Sony, and BMG Record Club operated by Bertelsman), and the Musical Heritage Society. The major label clubs offer a rather limited selection, focusing on the best-known works by major artists. You may enjoy your membership for a while, but you will soon be frustrated by the lack of selection. The Musical Heritage Society, on the other hand, has an enormous selection, including many lesser-known works. But the performers are not always top rank, although many are very talented and certainly more than adequate to do the job. It used to be that the Society licensed primarily European recordings from lesser-known labels, but now they are able to offer the same recordings found on the major labels.

All three clubs offer special bonuses when you join and require that you purchase a certain number of recordings per year. Also, they work on the "negative option" system; this means that if you don't return your reply card, you are automatically sent that month's selection. For some people, this turns into a major headache. Others quickly adjust to the rules and get quite a bit of enjoyment from the clubs. The clubs also publish newsletters that offer information on the recordings and composers. The clubs offer discounted prices and special bonuses to buyers who buy more than a certain number of discs, which can add up to additional savings. There are also direct-mail services of other kinds throughout the country that are not "clubs," but merely enable you to order through the mail; Bose Express Music is one of the best known. And you can always order directly from a record company or have your record store place an order for you.

There are some guidelines to follow in making your purchasing decisions. In this book, we focus on the CD format because the LP has gone the way of the 78 and cassettes are just too perishable for long-term listening pleasure. Compact-disc players can now be purchased for as little as $100, and a good machine with a remote control is only $50 or so more. CDs are now comparably priced to LPs, and they are more durable and have better sound quality. Sure, there are some purists who say LPs have a "warmer" sound, but let's face it, the average Joe can't tell the difference (although Joe's dog may hear the upper frequencies present on the CD)!

Now that we've decided to base our collection on CDs, there are several labels that specialize in classical music. Only a few years ago, we would have recognized these names as the leaders in classical-music recordings: Columbia Masterworks, RCA Red Seal, and Angel. The first two labels date back decades, with RCA Red Seal originating in the time of single-sided 78s, when the company was known as Victor Red Seal (c. 1910). However, foreign investors with their own agendas have gobbled up U.S. record labels, so we now have Sony Classical (for Columbia Masterworks) and BMG Classics (for RCA Red Seal), with only Angel remaining under its familiar name. However, it will take a while for the older titles to be replaced by new issues, so both CBS Masterworks and RCA Red Seal can still be found in many stores; BMG, to make matters more confusing, continues to issue recordings under both the RCA and BMG labels, and has also added Silver Seal (for budget releases) and Gold Seal (for extra-fancy releases) to the mix of names. Deutsche Grammophon, a division of Polygram, is the leading European classical label. Some of the more noteworthy "budget" labels are Nonesuch, Turnabout, Vanguard, and Vox. In this book, I have tried to limit my suggestions to the better-known labels, not because they are necessarily better than all the rest, but simply because they are easier to find in record stores and libraries. However, for some types of music (such as Early music), or to present a particular artist, I have some-times strayed further afield into European or smaller U.S. labels. Addresses are given for ordering information in Appendix A.

Name That Star!

Recordings allow us to experience the great classical musicians in our homes. They also allow us to capture the past. Although there are no recordings of Mozart performing, there are of Leo-nard Bernstein, Vladimir Horowitz, and Jascha Heifetz, to name just three legendary artists. Recordings ensure that their music will never die, and for some, the performer can be as important as the music (just as we value Little Richard's version of "Tutti Frutti" over Pat Boone's).

In selecting recordings for your home library, it's a good idea to stick to "tried-and-true" performers, orchestras, or quartets. To facilitate your learning curve, I've made a list of some of the better-known performers. This is by no means an exhaustive list, nor am I endorsing these performers over all others, past, present, or fu-ture. But these are the ones that have recorded most frequently, and you might find these to be reliable standbys when faced with a purchasing decision. For some of these names, I have listed anthology or celebratory recordings; you will, of course, find many more recordings by these artists throughout the book.

ORCHESTRAS

Here are some of the leading orchestras of the world, along with their current music directors (conductors). Note that they may have had other conductors and guest conductors in the past (represented on currently available recordings). Conductors come and go, but the quality of these orchestras has stayed relatively stable.

Bavarian Radio Symphony Orchestra: Sir Colin Davis, conductor
Berlin Philharmonic Orchestra: Claudio Abbado, conductor (headed for thirty-five years by Herbert von Karajan, who made over 800 recordings with the orchestra)

Boston Pops Orchestra: John Williams, conductor (Williams composed the music for *Star Wars* and other major motion pictures. He follows in the footsteps of the great conductor Arthur Fiedler, who led the Pops for forty-nine years)

Boston Symphony Orchestra: Seiji Ozawa, conductor

Chicago Symphony Orchestra: Daniel Barenboim, conductor (previously headed by the celebrated Sir Georg Solti, who holds the record for Grammy awards won by any performer in any musical field, at thirty)

Cleveland Orchestra: Christoph von Dohnanyi, conductor

Israel Philharmonic Orchestra: Zubin Mehta, music director

London Philharmonia Orchestra: Giuseppe Sinopoli, conductor

London Symphony Orchestra: Michael Tilson Thomas, conductor

Los Angeles Philharmonic: Esa-Pekka Salonen, conductor

New York Philharmonic Orchestra: Kurt Masur, conductor (the oldest active orchestra in the U.S., headed for many years by Leonard Bernstein)

Philadelphia Orchestra: Riccardo Muti, conductor (headed for many years by Eugene Ormandy)

Pittsburgh Symphony Orchestra: Lorin Maazel, conductor

Saint Louis Symphony Orchestra: Leonard Slatkin, conductor

San Francisco Symphony: Herbert Blomstedt, conductor

Recommended Listening

Two albums give you a chance to sample the Boston Pops, old and new. *Night on Bald Mountain* (Deutsche Grammophon 413689-2 GMF) is a typical program of well-loved classics by Fiedler and his gang, including works by Mussorgsky, Tchaikovsky ("Overture 1812"), Saint-Saëns ("Danse Macabre"), Khachaturian ("Sabre Dance"), Dukas ("The Sorcerer's Apprentice"), and Debussy ("Clair de Lune"). *By Request* (Philips 420178-2 PH) features the "new" Pops with John Williams at the helm, playing many of his famous movie themes.

Centennial Collection (RCA Gold Seal 60206-2-RG) is a three-CD set celebrating the 100th birthday of the Chicago Symphony. It features historic recordings made by all of the permanent conductors of the orchestra up to Solti, plus many notable guests, in a program of music by major 19th-century composers.

For fans of Leonard Bernstein and the New York Philharmonic,

Sony Classical has issued a ten-CD collection celebrating the Bernstein years. They are catalogued as Sony Classical SFK 46706-46715.

Music in a Romantic Mood (Odyssey MBK 38919) is a budget-priced collection featuring Eugene Ormandy conducting the Philadelphia Orchestra in a program of 19th-century favorites by Borodin, Ravel, Debussy, Rachmaninoff, and others.

The most prolific European conductor was Herbert von Karajan. He recorded so many works that it would be impossible to select a single representative disc. He is best known for his handling of German composers, particularly Beethoven. *Encores* (Deutsche Grammophon 413587-2 GH) features popular works by Liszt (the "Hungarian Rhapsody"), Rossini ("William Tell Overture"), and others. Although this is strictly an old-warhorse program, the CD gives a good introduction to this orchestra's sound. Deutsche Grammophon has issued a six-CD set of von Karajan's first recordings leading a number of different European orchestras (423525-2 GD06) for the true fan.

CHAMBER ORCHESTRAS

Chamber orchestras are smaller ensembles than full-scale orchestras. They are usually based on 17th- through early 19th-century ensembles and perform music of the Baroque through early Romantic eras. One of the pioneers of the chamber orchestra was Trevor Pinnock, who founded the well-loved English Concert to perform music of earlier periods in a more authentic setting. Some chamber orchestras also feature period instruments. Often the conductors of these groups double as instrumentalists, which was typical of the earlier orchestras that they are modeled after.

Academy of Saint Martin-in-the-Fields: Sir Neville Marriner, artistic director (one of the best-loved English chamber orchestras that has recorded prolifically)

Brandenburg Collegium: Anthony Newman, conductor and harpsichordist

Brandenburg Ensemble: Alexander Schneider, conductor

English Bach Festival Orchestra: Lina Lalandi, artistic director

English Chamber Orchestra: Pinchas Zukerman, conductor and soloist

English Concert: Trevor Pinnock, founder and music director
Los Angeles Chamber Orchestra: Iona Brown, music director
Orchestra of the Eighteenth Century: Frans Brüggen, director
St. Paul Chamber Orchestra: Christopher Hogwood, music director
Vienna Chamber Orchestra: Philippe Entremont, music director

Recommended Listening

The two most famous chamber orchestras are the Academy of
Saint Martin-in-the-Fields and the English Concert. Each has
recorded profusely; you'll find a good cross section of their recordings listed in the body of this book. To get a good comparison
of the orchestras' styles, compare their recordings of Bach's well-
loved Brandenburg Concerti (Academy of Saint Martin-in-the-
Fields, led by Marriner: Philips 40076-2 AH and 400077-2 AH;
the English Concert, led by Pinnock: Deutsche Grammophon
410500-2 AH and 410501-2 AH).

STRING QUARTETS

Budapest Quartet (an old standard)
Cleveland Quartet (staffed by members of the Cleveland Orchestra)
Colorado String Quartet
Emerson String Quartet (young quartet whose trademark is that the two violin-
     ists share the lead role)
Guarneri String Quartet
Juilliard String Quartet (the granddaddy of them all, one of the greatest, with a
     distinguished history)
Kronos Quartet (Egads, a punk string quartet! OK, they wear hip clothes and
     play hip music, but they're good musicians, too.)
Manhattan String Quartet (associated with the Manhattan School of Music)
Takacs String Quartet (Eastern European ensemble)
Tokyo String Quartet

Recommended Listening

It's always fun to compare the same works performed by different artists. Two of the greatest string quartets, the Juilliard and
the Guarneri, have recorded the complete Beethoven string quartets. Each set consists of nine CDs, so those deep of pocket can

purchase the entire work. For the thrifty, each package is broken into three sets of three CDs each, about the cost of a night's stay at Econo-Lodge (and a lot more relaxing!). The Juilliard CDs are cataloged as Columbia Masterworks M3K-37868; 37859; 37873. The Guarneri CDs are RCA Gold Seal 3-60456-2-RG; 3-60457-2-RG; 3-60458-2-RG.

PIANISTS

Vladimir Ashkenazy (also conducts the Berlin Radio Symphony)
Daniel Barenboim (conductor of the Chicago Symphony)
Leonard Bernstein (more famous as a composer and conductor)
Alfred Brendel (famous for his interpretation of Beethoven's piano works)
Van Cliburn (won instant fame for being the first American to win the prestigious Tchaikovsky International Competition in Moscow in 1958, at the height of the Cold War/Sputnik fever. Noted for his performances of the Romantic piano repertoire)
Alicia de Larrocha
Misha Dichter
Christoph Eschenbach (noted for his performances of Mozart's and Beethoven's piano music)
Glenn Gould (eccentric personality and pianist, noted for rarely playing in public and always wearing gloves when he performed! A unique and talented pianist)
Vladimir Horowitz (the long-lived virtuoso who some consider to be the greatest Romantic pianist ever)
Katia and Marielle Labeque (Canadian sisters who play a mix of classical and popular piano duets)
Ruth Laredo
Murray Perahia
André Previn (plays in both classical and jazz styles; noted for his popular film scores)
Artur Rubinstein (another legendary figure, noted for his performance of the Romantic repertoire, particularly Chopin)
Peter Serkin (appeared in long flowing robes in the mid-'70s during a Buddhist phase)
Rudolf Serkin (Peter's father; one of the finest pianists of our time and the founding director of the Marlboro Music Festival in Vermont until his death in May 1991)

Recommended Listening

The Alfred Brendel Collection (Vanguard 6-OVC-4015) is a varied program of Chopin, Liszt, Mozart, Schumann, Schubert, and others by this master pianist. Alicia de Larrocha honors her Spanish heritage on Spanish Fireworks (London 417795-2 LM), an album of works by noteworthy Spanish composers.

For tribute albums, there is The Glenn Gould Legacy, Volumes 2–4 (oddly, volume 1 is not available on CD; Columbia Masterworks M3K-39036, 42107, 42150). These three-CD sets proceed chronologically; the last volume is all 20th-century music.

Vladimir Horowitz and Murray Perahia are represented by Columbia Masterworks on two CDs with the same name, A Portrait (Horowitz: MK-44797; Perahia: MK-42448). Artur Rubinstein is represented by Highlights (RCA Gold Seal 60211-2-RG).

One of the more interesting concept albums is My First Recital by Ruth Laredo (ESS.A.Y. CD 1006), a program of well-known classical pieces of varying difficulty. This gives beginning through advanced piano students some idea of the kind of music they can play, and also makes for enjoyable listening.

VIOLINISTS

Eugene Fodor (fiery young violinist whose career was sidetracked by well-publicized problems with drugs)

Jascha Heifetz (legendary violinist of the 1930s through the 1960s)

Nigel Kennedy ("The Nige" is the latest sensation from England, with punk hairdo, top-twenty Vivaldi hits, and MTV videos)

Fritz Kreisler (recording star of the '20s–'30s noted for his virtuosic performances)

Yehudi Menuhin (began as child virtuoso; later a noted instrumentalist and conductor and popularizer of classical music)

Shlomo Mintz

Itzhak Perlman (Israeli violinist who has won great fame in the U.S.)

Nadja Salerno-Sonnenberg (fiery performer as famous for her low-cut gowns as her instrumental virtuosity)

Isaac Stern (violinist and champion of classical music credited with saving New York's Carnegie Hall)

Pinchas Zukerman

Recommended Listening

Heifetz was a prolific recording artist, from the "acoustic" period of recording (pre-1927) through the '40s. His earliest recordings can be heard on the three-CD set *The Acoustic Recordings* (RCA Gold Seal 3-0942-2-RG); later recordings can be heard on *The Decca Masters, Volumes 1 and 2* (MCA Classics MCAD 42211 and 42212).

To hear Fritz Kreisler, try *Legendary Performances* (RCA 5910-2-RC), drawn from recordings made in the '20s and '30s.

Itzhak Perlman has recorded many CDs of the classical standards, plus more popularly oriented ones. *Encores* (Angel CDC-54108) gives him a chance to shine on some bravura selections.

Isaac Stern has been honored with a four-CD compilation of his recordings made from 1946 through 1982 on *Celebration: Life with Music* (Columbia Masterworks M4K-42003).

CELLISTS

Pablo Casals (the first great virtuoso cellist of our time; also worked as a conductor)
Lynn Harrell
Yo-Yo Ma (a popular young performer)
Mstislav Rostropovich (Russian emigré noted for his fiery performances)

Recommended Listening

For early recordings of Casals, try *Encores* (Pearl GEMM CD 9263), drawn from late-'20s and '30s recordings. Yo-Yo Ma can be heard on *Portrait of Yo-Yo Ma* (Columbia Masterworks MK-44796), a sampler of his Columbia recordings.

FLUTISTS

James Galway (Irish virtuoso with a "twinkle in his eye")
Jean-Pierre Rampal (French flutist; one of the first to popularize the instrument as a soloist)
Eugenia Zukerman (also serves as classical-music correspondent for the CBS News program "Sunday Morning")

Recommended Listening

James Galway has made many recordings, some more popularly oriented than others. *The Classical James Galway* (RCA RCD1-7011) gives an overview of works by Mozart, Handel, Schubert, Vivaldi, J. S. Bach, and other well-known composers. *Portrait of Rampal* (Columbia Masterworks MK-42477) gives a similar overview of works by this noted flutist.

Pop Quiz #1: Test Your Classical-Music IQ

In the spirit of good fun, here's a classical-music quiz bound to stretch your IQ. Answers are found throughout the book (no cheating, please!) Take your time and circle the letter next to your answer for each question using a #2 pencil!

1. Antonio Vivaldi's nickname was
    (a) "the Red-Headed Fiddler"
    (b) "the Musical Priest"
    (c) "the Hard-Luck Blues Boy"
    (d) "the Red-Headed Priest"

2. An ancestor of the piano was
    (a) the clavichord
    (b) the clavicle
    (c) the rebec
    (d) the mund organ

3. Mozart's father was famous for writing
    (a) a Viennese sex manual, predating Freud by 200 years
    (b) the libretto for *The Magic Flute*
    (c) a violin instruction book, the first of its kind
    (d) *Women Who Love Men Who Can't Love Women*

4. J. S. Bach came from a distinguished family of
    (a) cattle ranchers
    (b) organ builders
    (c) organ players
    (d) origami champions

5. Isaac Stern is a violinist famous for
    (a) saving Carnegie Hall
    (b) saving the Carnegie Deli
    (c) swimming in Carnegie Lake
    (d) befriending Andrew Carnegie

6. The Baroque period is noteworthy for
    (a) a retreat from modal harmonies in search of fresh polyphony
    (b) a simplification of the fugue into its basic components
    (c) highly ornate melodic lines, often created on the spur of the moment by the soloist
    (d) the abandonment of instrumental styles in favor of a new age of *bel canto*

7. Oboe is to hautboy as clarinet is to
    (a) Charlemagne
    (b) samisen
    (c) chalumeau
    (d) Charles Guiteau

8. The pedalboard on the organ is used for
    (a) pumping the bellows
    (b) priming the engines
    (c) special effects, such as wah-wah and fuzztone
    (d) playing very low bass notes

9. Handel's "Water Music" was written to accompany
    (a) Mrs. Handel's singing in the shower
    (b) a rainy day on the Thames
    (c) the king's barge trip on the Thames from Whitehall
    (d) synchronized swimming at the 1708 Summer Olympics

10. Beethoven's third symphony was originally inspired by
    (a) Napoleon Bonaparte
    (b) the Duke of Wellington
    (c) Thomas Jefferson
    (d) Wolfgang Amadeus Mozart

Answers: 1 (d); 2 (a); 3 (c); 4 (c); 5 (a); 6 (c); 7 (c); 8 (d); 9 (c); 10 (a).

TWO
THE BASICS

The term "classical music" has been applied rather loosely to a wide variety of music created over the last 1,000 years or so in Europe and America. It is often used to describe anything from the chants of Medieval monks to the electronic burps and bleeps of modern music. Obviously, this is a rather broad definition that is only useful insofar as it sorts out the "classical" genre from pop, jazz, easy listening, and so forth.

Actually, this broadly defined classical music is usually divided into musical periods, one of which is called the "Classical era." These divisions are:

Early or Medieval (c. 1000–1400)
Renaissance (1400–1600)
Baroque (1600–1750)
Classical (1750–1820)
Romantic (1820–1900)
Modern (1900–today)

When most people describe "classical music," they usually are referring to music created in three of these periods: the Baroque, Classical, and Romantic eras. It is from these periods that the best-known composers come. It is also across this time frame, from

1600 to 1900, that modern musical instruments developed and new groupings of instruments (such as string quartets and orchestras) originated, new compositional forms were pioneered, and new theories of composition were formalized. This is the time period we will focus on in this book. But, in order to enhance our understanding of how music has developed, we will take a brief look at each musical period.

Early/Medieval Music

The first great musical instrument was the human voice, and so this first period of musical development emphasized vocal over instrumental music. Musical instruments of the era—such as recorders and small harps—were not as sophisticated as those introduced in later years, and so were more limited in their melodic capabilities. Early music focused on melodic, rather than harmonic, expression. One melody was performed at a time, often based on a simple mode rather than the modern scales. (Modes are scales created by the ancient Greeks and rediscovered in the Middle Ages. The notes in each mode have a unique relationship, so that a piece of music cannot be "transposed" or moved from one mode to another, as you can do with the modern scales. The modes also are not well suited to harmonic composition.)

The church was the major center of early musical performance and preservation. Monks would chant prayers at certain set times each day; these chants were called plainsong. Originally sung in unison, harmonizations began to come to this music toward the end of the era. Monks with lower voices would sing the melodic line an octave below (creating parallel octaves); those whose voices were not suited to either octave would sing a fifth above or below the primary melody (creating parallel-fifth harmonies).

At the court, musicians were part of the household staff, dedicated to entertaining the king and also serving an important role on ceremonial occasions. Trumpeters—playing simple one-note horns—could be counted on to play a ceremonial flourish when royalty entered the room. In some parts of Europe, bagpipers were used to lead men into battle; the pipe calls would announce the presence of specific regiments. The piper also was called on to compose victory anthems or laments for the loss of life when the battle fell short of victory. Harpers attended kings, playing small, simple harps (not like the modern concert harp). They would often compose poems that would recount the deeds of the king and set them to music. In this way, the history of a monarchy could be preserved.

Recommended Listening

"Early music" has become increasingly popular, and there are many recordings available; however, most focus on the Renaissance and later, because this music is more appealing to modern ears. The Clemencic Consort took an early-13th-century manuscript known as the *Carmina Burana* and has released it on a three-CD set (Harmonia Mundi HMA 190336.38). The work includes both sacred and secular songs and instrumental selections performed on period instruments. *Il Canto Goliardico Nel Medioevo* (Tactus TC 12012001) presents 12th- through 15th-century religious and secular songs, as might have been sung by students at the University of Bologna in Italy (the CD was issued to celebrate the university's 900th anniversary!).

There are many CDs available of Gregorian chants, particularly from Eastern Europe, where there are monks that still practice this ancient tradition. Paraclete has issued a sampler of Gregorian chants on CD-829. *Gregorian Chant from the Abbey of Kergonan* (Arion ARN 268101) is a two-CD set of chants for Easter and other special occasions performed by the choir of the Abbey of Sainte Anne de Kergonan. *Gregorian Chants from Hungary* (Hungaroton HCD-12559) gives you an idea of how this tradition has survived in Eastern Europe.

Some idea of early harp music can be gleaned from *Harp Collection* by Frances Kelly (Amon Ra CD SAR 36), featuring works from the 13th through the 19th centuries played on period instruments. *In a Medieval Garden* (Nonesuch N5-71120) by the Buetens Lute Ensemble presents 13th- through 15th-century selections.

Renaissance Music

A reawakening of interest in the arts and sciences spread from Italy in the late 15th century throughout Europe over a period of about 100 years. Greek and Roman learning was rediscovered, and many new discoveries were made in science, mathematics, geography, architecture, art, theater, and, of course, music. The Renaissance saw several new vocal forms come into vogue in both secular and sacred arenas. Hymns were long known in the church; they were used as part of the church service, usually with the entire congregation joining in to sing in unison. Motets, or elaborate part-songs, were introduced in the Renaissance; in the Protestant church, these became known as anthems. The madrigal was a secular form of the motet; in other words, it was a part-song sung by a group of voices, but usually its subject matter was drawn from mythology or courtly love poetry, rather than religious texts.

New musical instruments abounded. The viol family, forerunners of today's violins, replaced earlier bowed instruments. The lute, a bowl-backed instrument somewhat similar to today's guitar, was made in various styles and sizes to play in different ranges. Virginals, clavichords, and harpsichords became popular keyboard instruments for courtiers, with the organ coming into its own in churches.

This burst of new instrument development was inspired by a fundamental change in musical thinking. Whereas in the Medieval era music was more or less limited to a single melodic line, the notion of polyphony, or the performance of more than one melody at the same time, revolutionized musical composition. The introduction of a range of musical instruments in families (mirroring the vocal divisions in human beings from soprano to bass) enabled composers to begin thinking in terms of musical "parts," with each part complementing the other.

A further innovation was the gradual elimination of the modes in court music in favor of modern scales more suited to polyphonic writing (and eventually harmonic writing). There are two basic types of scales, major and minor. In each, the relationship among the notes is fixed, no matter what the starting tone. This makes transposition—or moving a melodic line from one "key" to another—simple, so that complementary parts can be written in the range of each instrument or vocalist.

Some of the key composers of the Renaissance include, in church music, Giovanni Palestrina (c. 1525–1594) of Italy and William Byrd (1543–1623) of England. Great Britain produced a number of noted keyboardists and composers, including Byrd, Giles Farnaby (c. 1563–1600), and Orlando Gibbons (1583–1625). The British courtiers became enthusiastic keyboardists, and many of the popular folk dances of the day were preserved in keyboard arrangements.

Several master church organists were active in this era, including Jan Pieterszoon Sweelinck (1562–1621) of Holland and Girolamo Frescobaldi (1583–1643) of Italy. Sweelinck was one of the first great writers of fugues (fugues and other compositional forms are discussed later in this chapter).

Music making in the Renaissance was beginning to spread well beyond the walls of the church. King Henry VIII was an avid musician and composer who collected some 381 instruments, 272 winds and 109 strings! Even beyond the court itself, the growing middle class was beginning to enjoy making music; wealthy merchants might own several sets of lutes or viols, enabling them to perform with and for their friends.

Recommended Listening

One of the best-known groups specializing in Renaissance music is the Waverly Consort; a good introduction to their work is *A Renaissance Christmas Celebration* (Columbia Masterworks MK-34554). Another starting place for this style of music is *A Renaissance Tour of Europe* (Dorian DOR 90133), giving an overview of forty works by twenty-one European composers. The Broadside Band (directed by Jeremy Barlow) has recorded several CDs of the popular dance music of the day on period instruments; they are all worth a listen: *Il Ballarino,* drawing from a collection of the same name from 1581 (Hyperion CDA 66244), presents Italian dance music of the 16th century; *Danses populaires françaises* (Harmonia Mundi HMC-90.1152) is a compendium of tunes from the famous 1589 book *Orchésographie* by Thoinot Arbeau, an early treatise on French court dance; and *John Playford's Popular Tunes* (Saydisc CDSAR-28) presents a selection from the well-known *English Dancing Master,* a series of books on English court dances of the Renaissance and Baroque eras published between 1651 and 1728.

Palestrina's setting of the "Stabat Mater" is available on MCA Classics MCAD-25191, performed by the Pro Cantione Antiqua. William Byrd's sacred vocal music can be heard performed by Chanticleer (a male vocal group) on Harmonia Mundi HMU-90.5182. His harpsichord works can be heard performed by Davitt Moroney on a Harmonia Mundi two-CD set, HMNC-901241/42. Jan Pieterszoon Sweelinck's organ works can be heard on Chandos CHAN 0514 performed by Piet Kee, along with works by Dietrich Buxtehude, a contemporary of Sweelinck's whose music influenced Bach.

Baroque Music

The Baroque period is most famous for its highly ornate compositions. Centered in Italy, the first Baroque composers were primarily writing vocal music and began their careers as musical revolutionaries. They rejected the polyphony of Renaissance music in favor of modern harmonizations based on the major and minor scales. They also emphasized melodic improvisation, creating great feeling through highly ornamented melodies. When polyphony returned in the late-Baroque era, the older modes had vanished and harmony became an integral part of polyphonic writing.

The Baroque era had several key composers. On the vocal side, Claudio Monteverdi (1567–1643) was the first composer to write an opera (*Orfeo* in 1607) and the first to write for a popular audience (his opera *Adone* was performed for a public audience in 1639; previously, all operas were bankrolled and performed for the sole delight of courtiers).

Monteverdi also revolutionized the orchestra. In *Orfeo,* composed and performed for his patron the Duke of Mantua, he employed an orchestra of forty pieces, of which the fifteen lead instruments were strings (viols and violins). This may simply have been a fluke: the Duke may have employed more string players than other instrumentalists, and Monteverdi undoubtedly had to work with what was at hand. But the fact that the strings were more prominent became a model for other orchestras, leading directly to the key role that the strings play in the modern orchestra.

The other key Italian Baroque composers were a group of violinists: Arcangelo Corelli (1653–1713), Antonio Vivaldi (1678–1741), Francesco Geminiani (1687–1762), and Giuseppe Tartini (1692–1770). They singlehandedly transformed the composition of string music, and also championed the modern violin over the older viol. We'll be discussing their music in some depth in the chapter on Baroque music.

Recommended Listening

We will be giving an in-depth listing of Baroque recordings in chapter 4. Some CDs that give an overview of this musical style are: *The Baroque Collection* (Vox/Turnabout PVTS 7601), a budget-priced overview of Baroque composers including Corelli, Couperin, Handel, Scarlatti, Telemann, and Vivaldi; *Baroque Masterpieces* (Enigma Classics D21C-74628), featuring Pachelbel's oft-recorded "Kanon" and works by J. S. Bach, Handel, Telemann, and Vivaldi; and *Great Baroque Favorites* (Columbia Masterworks MYK-38482), featuring many of the same composers.

For Monteverdi's *Orfeo*, try the London Baroque Ensemble's production on a two-CD set, Angel CDCB-47141, featuring period instruments.

Classical Music

The lines between the "Baroque" and "Classical" eras are somewhat blurred, with some scholars calling Bach a "late-Baroque" composer and others placing him squarely in the Classical period. The main distinction between the eras is that, while the Baroque emphasized surface beauty, the Classical developed new structures for musical works. These developments ranged from the intricacies of the fugue through the creation of longer compositional forms, such as the sonata and eventually the symphony.

One meaning of the word "classical" is balanced or symmetrical composition. In classical architecture, such as the Greek Parthenon, the elements are perfectly balanced. You can take a photograph of the building and fold it in half and find that each side perfectly mirrors the other. Similarly, in Classical music, compositional form becomes all important, with the ideas of balance, harmony, and complementary melodies being developed to their greatest degree.

We'll be spending a great deal of time discussing the great composers of this era, but for now we will simply mention a few of them: Johann Sebastian Bach, George Frideric Handel, Franz Joseph Haydn, and Wolfgang Amadeus Mozart.

Romantic Music

The Romantic era in the arts began as a reaction to the formality of the Classical period. After all, perfect balance and harmony is nice, but it doesn't leave a lot of room for composers to express emotions through their compositions. Stormy emotionalism became a hallmark of Romanticism carried to its ultimate expression.

The Romantic composers were also writing almost entirely for a paying audience of middle-class concertgoers. Whereas in the past the court and church were the primary sponsors for music, the nobility and clergy were increasingly challenged politically and financially. As democratic or semidemocratic societies replaced the old aristocracies, musicians increasingly relied on the public forum. They became true performers as well as composers. Mozart certainly began this trend, although his performances were still pretty much within the confines of the courts. But Beethoven, Liszt, Chopin, and Mendelssohn were all popular performers as well as composers, and their music had to appeal to popular taste. This may be another reason why Romantic music became overtly emotional, because high emotions appeal more to listeners than rigorous symmetry.

Modern Music

The music of the 20th century in many ways is a continuation of the struggle between the Classical and Romantic styles. Some composers have championed highly theoretical music, exploring twelve-tone and other esoteric scales based on advanced music theory. Others have continued to explore musical feelings, championing a popular music expression aimed squarely at the concert audience. New technologies—such as electronic musical instruments and tape recorders—have expanded the music-making possibilities.

A common argument heard against modern classical music is that the music makers have left the audience behind, or even disdain it. John Cage's famous "playing the audience," where he sits totally still at a piano keyboard for many minutes hoping to elicit a reaction from his listeners, is considered either a brilliant tour de force exploring the relation of audience to performer or a slap in the face of the musical public.

Modern experimental music certainly hasn't captured a large listening public. But, then again, this music wouldn't be experimental if it immediately appealed to everyone! It will take many years before we can judge the success of this style.

Recommended Listening

Joshua Pierce has recorded two CDs of John Cage's music for piano and prepared piano, issued on Wergo CD-60151-50 and 60157-50.

Philip Glass is currently very popular for his hypnotically repetitive music; his opera *Einstein on the Beach*, performed by the Glass Ensemble under his direction, is available on a four-CD set on Columbia Masterworks M4K-38875. *Songs from Liquid Days* (Columbia Masterworks MK-39564) features lyrics to Glass's melodies by popular songwriters such as Paul Simon and David Byrne.

The more traditional 20th-century composers include Aaron Copland, whose "Appalachian Spring" (composed for Martha Graham's dance of the same name) is a perennial favorite; it can be heard along with related dance music ("Billy the Kid," "Rodeo," and "Fanfare for the Common Man") performed by the New York Philharmonic under the direction of Leonard Bernstein on Columbia Masterworks MK-42265. George Gershwin was a popular songwriter who wrote several jazz-flavored classical works. Arthur Fiedler leads the Boston Pops in interpretations of Gershwin's two most famous works, "An American in Paris" and "Rhapsody in Blue," on RCA Red Seal AGK1-5215.

Musical Forms

Writing a single melody to be sung or played on an instrument is not too hard. But as soon as you begin composing for a group, a question arises: how can you accommodate the various voices? You could have everyone sing or play the same part, but this quickly proves tiresome. Plus, some people may find the music outside of their vocal or instrument's range, so that the composer has to do something to accommodate them.

One way to alleviate the monotony of playing a simple melody over and over again is to introduce variations, or elaborations on the basic melody or theme. Now everybody is playing the same thing, but at least that theme changes as the piece progresses. In theory, there could be as many variations as the composer could imagine. But eventually melodic ideas are exhausted, and the "one-thing-after-another" form is rather uninteresting to the listener.

Composers solved this problem by creating various forms of counterpoint. Counterpoint literally means "point against point." In music, it is the placing of two or more melody lines against each other to create a single work. Two common forms of counterpoint are the canon and fugue.

CANONS AND FUGUES

In the canon, or round, everyone sings or plays the same melody, but they do not all start at the same time. A simple four-part canon can be created by having one person start to play the melody, followed by a second person entering after two measures, a third person after four measures, and a fourth after six measures. Each performer does not have to learn a difficult part, but the overall creation is more intricate than the individual parts. Think of your experience in grade school singing "Three Blind Mice." Although the melody is simple, and each person sings the same melody in the same key, the overall round is complex. Without too much effort, you've created a polyphonic composition.

A fugue is a highly developed canon. Many Baroque and Classical fugues were divided into two parts: the exposition and the episode. The exposition is the major part of the fugue in which the counterpoint is worked out. A subject, or short melody, is introduced by a single instrumental voice. Then, this subject is repeated by the various voices as they enter, although it may not be repeated in the same key. Meanwhile, the first voice will perform a countersubject, a continuation or elaboration of the initial subject, designed to complement it. The episode serves as a respite from the counterpoint of the exposition. Usually in a different key, it may be either based on the original subject or introduce an entirely different one. In either case, the episode usually features far less counterpoint than the exposition.

Longer fugues were made simply by stringing together expositions followed by episodes: exposition-episode-exposition-episode-exposition-episode, and so forth. Composers also developed a more complex form called the double fugue. There are two types of double fugues: the most common is one in which the countersubject is so distinctive that it is easily recognized by the listener. The composer treats it almost as a separate melody, rather than just a development of the original subject, so that it becomes in a sense a second subject. Rarer are the double fugues that consist of two complete fugues put together into a single composition.

FROM SUITE TO SYMPHONY

While the fugue is an interesting form, composers eventually tired of it, and listeners were often lost in the nooks and crannies of theme and development. As composers became more interested in composing harmonized music, polyphony faded as a key compositional element. New ways of making a music composition were needed.

When composers began to write for the lute or virginal, they drew on the popular repertoire of dance music and songs, well-known melodies that many people wished to play. Creating simple or complex harmonizations for these tunes was a favorite pastime of Renaissance composers, and many harmonized books of popular dances and songs were compiled for the use of courtiers and the wealthier classes. But as composers and musicians grew more proficient, these short dance and song melodies again proved tiresome; you were simply playing the same thing over and over again. How could a longer composition be created?

The suite is a simple solution to this problem; here the composer grouped together a series of dance melodies to form a longer whole. The composition opened with a commanding piece of music to gain the attention of the audience, called an overture. These overtures often became quite complex, and later gained a life of their own, leading to further innovations in composition. Following the overture in the suite were a series of popular dance forms, such as allemandes, courantes, gigues, minuets, or sarabandes. The dances were often performed in groups of two, so that one minuet would be played followed by a second in a contrasting key or mood to complement the first. The first would then return to finish the movement. This A-B-A format is found in later forms such as the sonata, concerto, and symphony. Suites were composed for single instruments, quartets, or larger ensembles.

In the 18th century, the sonata form was created, which lay the basis for all classical composition of the next 200 years. This form took the notion of two contrasting themes (A and B) and built on it to create an entire work. The sonata is usually written in three contrasting movements. Within each movement, there are three contrasting parts. For example, the first movement opens with a theme, usually in a fast rhythm, followed by a slower, contrasting melody, and closing with a recapitulation of the first theme. Clever composers used theories of harmony to add further contrast: the first theme might be in a major key (G major, for example), and the second would be written in the relative minor (E minor, in this example). The same theory would be applied to the movements themselves: the first movement predominantly in a major key, played in a quick rhythm, the second movement in a contrasting minor key, played in a slow rhythm, followed by a third movement in the original key.

The difference between a sonata, concerto, and symphony has to do with the number of instruments involved in the performance. In the 18th-century sonata, usually one to five instruments played. The concerto featured a single instrument or group of instruments playing a theme, followed by an entire orchestra playing a countertheme (we'll discuss this in more detail when we study the music of Arcangelo Corelli in chapter 4). The symphony featured a large number of instruments, all playing together.

The symphony reached its maturity in the mid-18th through mid-19th centuries, when the compositional techniques of the sonata were applied to orchestral works. Composers such as Mozart, Haydn, and Beethoven used the A-B-A structure of the sonata to add dramatic tension to their symphonies. They also appreciated the differences among the various instruments, and used them to full advantage to create special tonalities and textures within the orchestra. The drama and variety of their compositions gave the symphony new depths of expression and feeling.

Classical Music Goes to the Movies

Hollywood has, from time to time, created film biographies of famous composers. Those of you familiar with film biographies of jazz musicians know just how silly these Hollywoodizations can be (in *The Glenn Miller Story*, made in 1954, Jimmy Stewart spends a good deal of time "looking for a sound"). But, they do feature good music (sometimes) and are fun for all their dopiness.

The Great Waltz (1938; 1972): Two film biographies of Johann Strauss, sharing the same title. The 1938 version has lovely music but a rather dippy Hollywood love triangle. The 1972 version is fun only because it is so bad; the same filmmaker also butchered Edvard Grieg's life in *Song of Norway*.

A Song to Remember (1945): Biography of Frédéric Chopin directed by the great Charles "King" Vidor and featuring the lovely Merle Oberon as George Sand. Music is enjoyable but plot is thin.

More recently, Chopin, George Sand, Liszt, and other 19th-century artists were featured in the fictionalized film *Impromptu* (1991). Although not a "true" story, the film does give insights into the unusual relationships among the characters, plus a vivid picture of French intellectual society of the day. Australian actress Judy Davis and American musical star Mandy Patinkin lead a talented cast.

Song of Love (1947): The story of those fun-loving Schumanns, featuring Katharine Hepburn as Mrs. S., Paul Henreid as her spouse, and Robert Walker as Brahms! Hollywood pulls out the stops in a "serious" production that plods rather than thrills.

Song without End (1960) is a fairly standard Hollywood-bio of composer Franz Liszt. It features a distinguished cast, including Dirk Bogarde in the title role, and lavish settings. The score won an Oscar, and is one of the finer uses of classical music in the movies. Film buffs will be interested to know that this was the last film made by legendary director Charles "King" Vidor; he died during the making of the film, and was replaced by another Hollywood legend, George Cukor.

Song of Norway (1970): A biography of Edvard Grieg in which pretty vistas don't make up for a plot that strays far from the truth. Features weak, abridged musical excerpts from the composer's canon.

Director Ken Russell, of the "excess-is-more" school of filmmaking, has made several feature films and television biographies of musicians. These include 1970's *The Music Lovers,* on a year in the lives of Tchaikovsky and Mahler, and 1975's *Lisztomania* (winning the unlikely casting award with Roger Daltrey of the Who portraying that wild and crazy guy Franz Liszt and featuring Beatle drummer Ringo Starr in a supporting role). Russell's TV miniseries include the stories of Verdi and Wagner. If you can bear Russell's overly active camerawork, and his penchant for playing fast and loose with the facts, these films can be fun.

Amadeus (1984): Milos Foreman's adaptation of the hit Broadway play that pits virtuous Salieri against girl-crazy Mozart. Lots of great music in this film, and F. Murray Abraham deservedly won an Oscar for his portrayal of the bitter Salieri, although Tom Hulce's Mozart has a serious case of the giggles. Not historically accurate, but fun.

Fans of animation need no reminder that one of the greatest classical-music films of all time is Walt Disney's *Fantasia* (1940), featuring many beloved melodies: "The Sorcerer's Apprentice," featuring Mickey Mouse's battle with the dancing brooms; "The Dance of the Hours," with balletic hippos and alligators; "The Rite of Spring," set in prehistoric dinosaur days; and "A Night on Bald Mountain," featuring the memorable Chernobog, one of Disney's greatest villains. Disney went to town with this production, featuring the great Leopold

Stokowski conducting the Philadelphia Orchestra in an early stereophonic recording. Only a minor success when it was first released, *Fantasia* became a cult classic among '60s hippies who thought it was the ultimate "trip." Today it is a venerable family classic.

Less well known is the Italian animated classic *Allegro Non Troppo,* made in 1976 by Bruno Bozzetto. Despite rather inane live-action comedy sequences, this has some charming animation and features the music of Debussy, Dvořák, Vivaldi, and Stravinsky, among others. In one of the most imaginative sequences, Bozzetto presents a vision of human evolution using the music of Ravel's "Bolero." Worth searching out on videocassette.

Conductor Leopold Stokowski had a brief career in front of the camera, believe it or not. He appeared in the lively comedy *One Hundred Men and a Girl* (1937), in which Deanna Durbin charms the conductor into employing her out-of-work father and his musician cronies. The film alternates '30s screwball comedy with lovely musical sequences. In the less memorable *Carnegie Hall* (1947), a slew of noteworthy musicians join Stokowski—including Artur Rubinstein, Jascha Heifetz, Lily Pons, and Bruno Walter—as he leads the New York Philharmonic in a ditsy story of a backstage mom and her piano-playing son. How do you get to Carnegie Hall? Not this way . . .

Several movies have made effective use of classical scores, most notably *2001: A Space Odyssey* (1968), with its dramatic use of Richard Strauss's "Also Sprach Zarathustra." Stanley Kubrick's *A Clockwork Orange* (1971) introduced classical music to many rock fans; the soundtrack is still available on Warner Brothers BS 2573-2, featuring Walter/Wendy Carlos's synthesized versions of many famous classical works. For the life of a classical performer, there is Jack Nicholson in the 1970 existential tragedy *Five Easy Pieces.* Although more of a yarn of a lost young man than strictly a classical-music story, there is some nice piano playing here, plus the unforgettable Nicholson method for ordering toast from a recalcitrant diner waitress.

Also noteworthy is Ingmar Bergman's *Autumn Sonata* (1978), the last film made by Ingrid Bergman, who stars as an aging concert pianist who seeks to reconcile herself with her daughter, played by Liv Ullmann. The classic love story *Intermezzo* (1939) features romantic heartthrob Leslie Howard as a concert violinist who falls in love with his protégée, played by Ingrid Bergman in her first English-language role (she had played the same part in an earlier Swedish film); this was remade in 1980 as the honky-tonkin' *Honeysuckle Rose,* with Willie Nelson starring as the successful musician.

On the comedy front, there is Preston Sturges's delightful *Unfaithfully Yours*

(1948), starring Rex Harrison as a conductor who imagines that his attractive young wife is cheating on him. While leading the orchestra, he imagines different ways of ending his problem, in a series of hysterical comic situations. This is not to be confused with the 1984 remake of the same title, featuring a sour Dudley Moore as the orchestra leader.

THREE
THE INSTRUMENTS
OF CLASSICAL MUSIC

The classical-music revolution couldn't have happened without a series of new musical instruments and groupings of instruments into ensembles. While many homes have a piano today, the piano itself is only about 300 years old (just a drop in the bucket, musically speaking) and was only beginning to be known in the days of Bach and Mozart. The modern violin is also a relatively recent innovation, championed by a group of Italian musicians and instrument builders in the 17th and 18th centuries. Even the orchestra came into being fairly recently, and only in the last seventy-five years has it had a fixed form.

Fiddle Fever

The violin first appeared on the scene in the early 1500s, but it did not become widely accepted until the late 1700s. It took a group of instrumentalists (including Corelli, Vivaldi, and Geminiani) and talented builders (including Amati, Guarneri, and the celebrated Stradivarius) to make several innovative changes in the design and playing of earlier bowed, stringed instruments to create the modern violin.

Predecessors of the violin include various folk instruments, known as "fidils" or "feydils" (the predecessor of today's "fiddle") and the courtly "viol." Although the viol has a name similar to the violin's, it really is quite a different musical instrument. The viol was played in an upright position, resting on the knees or between the legs. Rather than playing individual notes, the instrument was designed so that several strings could easily be played at once, for the purpose of playing chords. Additionally, the fingerboard had frets, or fixed markers, so that individual notes could be played clearly. The viola da gamba, roughly equivalent in range to today's cello, was the main melody instrument in a viol ensemble.

Through the work of instrumentalists and craftsmen, the viol was transformed into the violin. The violin is the melody instrument in the string quartet (two violins, viola, and cello). It is held under the chin, making it easier to play farther up the neck than is possible on the viol (viol players rarely went beyond what is called "first position" by violinists today). The fretless fingerboard made playing slides, tremolo, vibrato, and other special effects possible, but also called for greater technical virtuosity by the violinist. A curved bridge meant that each note was separated; although it was still possible to play two notes (double-stops) or more at once for chords, the main emphasis was now on playing individual melody notes.

Of course, all of these changes did not occur at once. Rather, gradual improvements were made in the engineering of the instrument that led to changes in technique. The fingerboard was widened, making it easier to fret individual notes; the bridge was gradually arched, for the same purpose. The interior of the instrument was redesigned, incorporating tone bars so that the volume was increased. Its shape was refined for the purpose of improving tone. The tension on the strings, which had been rather loose on the viol, was tightened for greater control, clarity, and improved tone. The marriage of talented builders with enthusiastic musicians brought about these remarkable changes in a single generation, culminating in the Stradivarius violins that have served as the model for all violins made to this day.

Musicians, being a conservative lot, did not overwhelmingly embrace the violin. It took talented performers to convince the musical world that the violin deserved to replace the viol. Meanwhile, the popular viola da gamba continued to be played even after the rest of the viol family had been discarded; it has enjoyed a revival in today's Early-music circles. But as the repertoire expanded for the new family of instruments, the violin eventually became the most important voice in the classical family, taking the lead in the modern symphony orchestra.

Recommended Listening

It is difficult to find CDs that feature the viol family instruments in a solo capacity. However, many Early music/Baroque ensembles use these instruments in their groups. *Popular Masterworks of the Baroque* (Reference RR-13CD), performed by the group Tafelmusik on period instruments, features viol family instruments in a program of Bach, Purcell, Vivaldi, Telemann, and Pachelbel. Many of the recordings listed in chapter 2 following the Early music and Renaissance sections feature period instruments, including viol family members. Many great violin works are listed in the following chapters; in chapter 1 we gave listings for some of the most well-known violinists.

Kitten on the Keys

The pianoforte (or more simply, the piano) is the leading keyboard instrument today, although it is only about 300 years old and did not come into widespread use until the beginning of the 19th century. The organ is the most venerable member of the keyboard family, dating back about 1,000 years, with the harpsichord and, to a lesser extent, the clavichord taking the lead in the Baroque and Classical eras. In fact, the "piano" music of Bach and Mozart was primarily composed for organ or harpsichord.

The organ has always been associated with church music; large organs were too expensive and too expansive to fit into the average home! The harpsichord, on the other hand, was a courtier's instrument, and so was devoted to secular music. Not surprisingly, the repertoires for these instruments follow this natural division, with much of the great church music being composed for the organ and secular dance tunes being played on the harpsichord.

The first organs were relatively simple affairs. A single set of pipes was mounted in a small box with air power supplied by external bellows. When a key was pressed, a valve was opened allowing a single pipe to sound. These portable organs were often used in church processionals or parades and were given the name "portative organs."

For large churches, there was a need for bigger organs that could fill the hall with sound. Ambitious churchmen wished to have the most glorious organs, and so master builders began devising ways to get more sound from a single instrument. Additional keyboards (manuals) could be added, each operating additional sets of pipes. Or, a single keyboard could be used to control more than one set of pipes through the means of connecting tubing (couplers). An organist might want to add or subtract different sets of pipes to change the tone quality; this could be achieved by mechanical stops, which acted like traffic cops, controlling which set of pipes would sound when a key was depressed.

Soon, superlarge and supercomplicated organs were being made that could not be played by a single musician. Some were so large that it took several men simply to operate the bellows to supply the air needed to drive the enormous pipes. In one organ, two men stood on sets of bellows, rocking their feet back and forth in order to build enough air pressure to enable the instrument to play. In another, the keys were so large and heavy that the organist had to use his fist to make the note sound!

Just as the Italians led in the field of violin making, the Germans were the greatest organ builders. They came up with several engineering improvements leading to the modern organ. In the mid-17th century, the Germans introduced the pedalboard, a foot-activated keyboard used to operate the magnificent bass pipes of the organs. Without this and other design improvements, Bach's great organ works could never have been written.

The harpsichord enjoyed its greatest popularity in the period from 1500 to 1750. Actually, there are three distinct types of harpsichords: the virginal, spinet, and true harpsichord, differing primarily in their mode of construction. The virginal came first, and the other two variants evolved from it, with the true harpsichord eventually replacing its two earlier siblings.

In the piano, the strings are struck by hammers; in the harpsichord, the strings are plucked by picks or plectra. When you press down a key, a tiny piece of wood (called a jack) rises up. On its tip is mounted a piece of quill or leather that picks the string. As the jack falls back to place, an escapement prevents the pick from plucking the string a second time (otherwise, each time you pressed on a key you would hear the note sounding twice).

The virginal is a small rectangular box that is placed on a table top to be played (some fancier instruments have their own legs). Its single set of strings runs parallel to the longer side of the box. In the spinet, the strings are turned to a 45-degree angle from the keyboard, allowing for longer bass strings and a more powerful tone. In the harpsichord proper, the strings are turned to a 90-degree angle from the keyboard (just as they are in today's grand piano). Most harpsichords feature more than one set of strings, which the player can control either by opening stops (levers) or through pedals (foot controls). A second keyboard (or manual) was originally added to give the instrument greater range; in later harpsichords, the second keyboard allowed the player to play louder by adding additional strings to the notes played on the main keyboard. By switching between the two keyboards, the player could get a "forte" (loud) and "piano" (soft) effect.

The harpsichord had one major disadvantage: its tone was fixed by the nature of its mechanical design. No matter how hard you press on a harpsichord's key, you cannot vary the volume of the tone produced, nor can you manipulate the quality of the sound. By cleverly using stops, pedals, and additional keyboards, you can get some variety, but you are limited by the inherent design of the instrument.

The clavichord, an instrument popular from the 1300s through the 1800s, allowed the player to vary the volume and quality of the tone through a fluke of design. Instead of producing sounds by plucking the strings, the strings were struck from below by small pieces of metal called tangents. By varying pressure on the keys, a talented player could produce louder or softer tones. A crude tremolo, or vibrating sound, could also be produced by rocking on the key; this caused the tangent to strike the string many times in rapid succession. The clavichord suffered from one major limitation: its sound was delicate and soft, limiting its use to the home rather than the concert hall.

Toward the end of the 17th century, a variety of instrument builders were experimenting with keyboard instruments that would combine the best qualities of the harpsichord and the clavichord. They hoped to build an instrument with sufficient volume to be heard in a larger hall, but also with the clavichord's capabilities to alter tone and volume. Although many tried, the Italian Bartolommeo Cristofori (1665–1731) is generally credited with the breakthrough that led to the first pianoforte (or "soft-loud") in 1709.

Cristofori replaced the plectra of the harpsichord with small hammers that struck the strings from underneath. But a problem immediately arose: If the player held down the key to make the hammer strike the string, the hammer would stop the string from vibrating freely. Similarly, when the player released the key, the hammer would fall, but the vibration in the string would continue indefinitely, drowning out other notes. The answer was an ingenious system of escapements and dampers. The escapement regulated the movement of the hammer so that it dropped away from the string immediately after striking it; in this way, the vibration of the string would not be impeded. The damper was activated when the player released a key; it immediately dropped onto the string, stopping its vibration so that the next notes could be clearly heard.

Cristofori's first piano resembled a harpsichord in the design of its box, with the strings running at a 90-degree angle to the keyboard to allow for longer bass strings for better volume and tone. But, his piano was limited to a range of only four and a half octaves. It would take the piano 150 years to gain today's full seven-and-a-half-octave range. This is something to keep in mind when studying the piano music of Mozart, who played a piano with only a five-octave range, and Beethoven, who was limited to six octaves.

As Cristofori's invention spread, first to Germany and then to France and England, several improvements were made. One of the most important was the introduction of the loud, or sustain, pedal. This enabled the player to remove the dampers from all of the strings to give added sustain to the notes. The first pianists, centered in Italy and Vienna, favored a playing style similar to that used on the harpsichord: they used a light, crisp touch and did not vary the volume very much between loud and soft. Mozart probably played in this style. A rival school grew up in England around the playing of composer, instrument builder, and performer Muzio Clementi (1752–1832). Clementi played in a lyrical, flowing style, taking advantage of the piano's unique design, allowing for a greater and more expressive use of tone and volume. He was quite influential not only through his playing but through the pianos that he built, which incorporated further improvements in range and dynamics. Beethoven and the Romantic pianists who followed him (Chopin, Liszt) were greatly influenced by his innovations.

Much of the keyboard music that we associate today with the piano was actually written for the harpsichord, or occasionally the clavichord. Bach, Scarlatti, and Handel couldn't compose for the piano because it was either not yet invented or virtually unknown to them. Similarly, Mozart's and Haydn's early keyboard works were written for harpsichord. The first great pianist/composer was Beethoven, and his works set the stage for the explosion of piano compositions in the 19th century.

Recommended Listening

An overview of the music of many of the most famous historical organs still found in European churches can be heard on the six-CD set *Historical Church Organs of Europe* (Harmonia Mundi HMA-290060). Truly for the organ maniac, it is at least reasonably priced at a suggested retail of approximately the usual cost of two CDs! There are many other recordings of historical organs, including Jennifer Bate playing a selection of 18th-century English organ works on *From Stanley to Wesley, Volume 1* (Denon C37-7200); André Isoir's *Airs and Dances of Old Europe* (Pierre Vernay PV-787031), featuring Isoir playing a late-18th-century Eastern European organ; and Donald Joyce's *The Organ in Santa Prisca*

(Titanic Ti-187), celebrating a recently restored mid-18th-century Spanish organ found in Mexico.

For harpsichord, clavichord, and other early keyboard instruments, there is a plethora of good listening. Richard Burnett plays a number of early keyboards, including virginal, spinet, clavichord, harpsichord, chamber organs, and historical pianos, on *Keyboard Collection* (Amon Ra SAR CD-6), with a selection of works by Thomas Arne, Bach, Beethoven, Chopin, Clementi, Mozart, Schubert, and many others, giving an overview of styles from the 17th through 19th centuries. John Henry's *The Harpsichord 1689–1789* (Victoria VCD 19013) focuses on works from "the golden age" of harpsichord music, including works by Bach, F. Couperin, Handel, D. Scarlatti, and others. Gustav Leonhardt's *Clavichord Recital* (Philips 422349-2 PH) is a well-recorded and interesting selection of works performed on this under-recorded instrument. Trevor Pinnock, the well-known Early-music scholar, has recorded several excellent harpsichord albums, including *The Harmonious Blacksmith* (Deutsche Grammophon ARC-413591-2 AH).

For the piano and its repertory, we will be discussing individual works throughout the book; in chapter 1, we listed some recordings of well-known pianists. For those unafraid of owning the crassly titled *Greatest Hits of the Piano* (Columbia Masterworks MLK-45627, 45628, 45629), there is a cornucopia of well-known works here by Bach, Beethoven, Mozart, Brahms, and friends, performed by Glenn Gould, Philippe Entremont, Lazar Berman, Leon Fleisher, Rosalyn Tureck, and other artists who recorded for Masterworks over the last thirty years.

Woodwinds and Horns

Many of the instruments that we associate with classical music—the flute, trumpet, clarinet, oboe—did not exist in their current form until fairly recently (within the last 150 years). Understanding how earlier forms of these instruments were played can give us a better appreciation of the compositions written for them by Bach, Mozart, Handel, and Haydn.

FLUTES

The earliest form of the flute is still played today. It is the recorder, commonly used by school-age children as a first instrument. As you probably know, the recorder is an endblown flute; this means that the player blows into one end. A small notch in the mouthpiece breaks up the player's breath into pulses, creating the vibrating column of air that makes the sounds. Recorders have been around since at least the Medieval era and have been made in a variety of sizes to play in different ranges.

The first transverse, or sideblown, flutes were introduced in the early 18th century. In this design, a small hole is drilled in the side of a long, thin cylinder. By blowing across this hole, the player creates a vibrating column of air, which in turn makes the flute's sounds. The earliest flutes featured six open finger holes; by sliding the fingers across them, the flutist could achieve a variety of effects, including slides, trills, and half tones. Commonly these flutes were made of wood, giving them a mellow tone. Makers continued to refine the design of these instruments into the 19th century, adding keys that extended the flute's range. This type of flute is still commonly used in Irish traditional music, giving us an idea of the playing style that might have been heard in Bach's and Mozart's times.

It wasn't until the 1830s that the modern keyed flute was introduced with the Boehm system of fingering, named for German flutist Theobald Boehm (1793–1881). In earlier open-hole flutes, the holes were positioned for ease of fingering. However, the notes that these flutes produced were slightly out of tune when compared to a true scale. If you moved the holes to create an acoustically correct scale, it would be difficult to finger the instrument. Boehm's ingenious solution was to use a system of keys and levers to make it possible to have the holes in the correct places while keeping the keys directly under the fingers for easy playing. By the 1840s, the Boehm system was universally recognized as superior and had replaced the earlier design in the classical concert hall. One disadvantage to the Boehm system was that the notes were now fixed; the player could no longer slide into notes or embellish them with half tones or quarter tones as was possible in the open-hole design.

Originally, Boehm-system and earlier style flutes were made of wood and had a mellow tone. With the introduction of the Boehm system, the metal or silver flute gained popularity. These flutes have a sharper, brighter tone than wooden ones. This meant that they could be heard more easily in large groups, leading to a greater acceptance of the flute in orchestral ensembles.

Recommended Listening

René Clemencic plays a variety of different recorders on *Plays 21 Recorders* (Harmonia Mundi HMA-190384), in a program of Renaissance and Baroque music. To hear the recorder in a variety of musical styles, try Michala Petri's *Music from 1500–1900* (RCA 7749-2-RC), featuring harpsichord and cello accompaniment.

Stephen Preston can be heard playing 18th- and 19th-century flutes on *Flute Collection* (Amon Ra SAR CD-19) with keyboard accompaniments. Irish traditional musicians continue to play the wooden or open-hole flute to this day, and their playing style gives us an idea of what classical flute playing might have sounded like some 200 to 300 years ago. For the adventurous, you might try master Irish flutist Matt Malloy's *Stoney Steps* (Green Linnet GLCD 3041); Malloy is flutist for the popular Irish band The Chieftains.

THE OBOE

The double-reed oboe has a long string of forebears in instruments dating back at least to Roman times. In the 16th century, a family of instruments called shawms, pommers, and bombardes were popular double reeds. By the 17th century, the French hautboy and the bassoon made up the double-reed family. By the time of Mozart, the modern oboe and bassoon were more or less developed, although the instruments continued to be improved into the 19th century.

The oboe is unique in two design features: it has a conically shaped tube, i.e., its body flares out from the mouthpiece to the bell (as opposed to the clarinet and flute, which are cylindrical), and it produces its sound through the beating of a double reed. A double reed consists of two thin pieces of cane. The player puts the entire double reed into his or her mouth. By blowing on it, the reeds are brought into vibration and beat against each other. This beating motion opens and closes the column of air, causing a vibration in it, which is the source of the oboe's unique sound.

Early hautboys had a piercing or grating sound, and were limited in use primarily to military functions and special effects in orchestration. Bach used the oboe in his orchestrations to add additional punch to a series of notes, much as a composer might use the trumpet or other brass instruments today (in Bach's time, the trumpet was a much more limited instrument melodically than the oboe). By the time of Mozart and Haydn, the modern oboe was coming into general use. With the improvements in the instrument's design, composers were able to write melodic parts for it that would have been impossible to perform on the earlier versions of the instrument.

There is an entire family of oboe instruments, the best known being the oboe and the bassoon (or bass oboe). Falling below the oboe in pitch are the oboe d'amore and the cor anglais (or English horn), roughly corresponding to the viola and cello in a string quartet. The bassoon makes the bass, and the double bassoon corresponds to the double bass. There are many other oboe variants that have surfaced over the years, including the tenoroon (a small bassoon pitched a fourth or fifth higher than the normal bassoon), the heckelphone (falling in pitch between the cor anglais and the bassoon, and introduced by a German inventor named Heckel in 1905), and the sarrusophone (a family of double-reed instruments made of brass, introduced with limited success in the mid-19th century as brass replacements for the oboe and bassoon by a French bandleader named Sarrus).

Recommended Listening

Robin Canter plays a variety of oboes from the 13th through 19th centuries on *Oboe Collection* (Amon Ra SAR CD-22). *Famous Oboe Concertos* (Astoria DP 87014) features Senia Trubashnik playing well-known oboe works by Vivaldi, Handel, Bellini, Albinoni, and others.

The Amon Ra label has also issued a CD of period music on

bassoons, called the *Bassoon Collection* (SAR CD-35), featuring Frances Eustace and Andrew Watts playing period instruments in a program of music by Mozart, Elgar, Speer, Bertoli, and others.

THE CLARINET

The clarinet is a single-reed instrument, as opposed to the double-reed oboe. In this case, a single thin reed of cane is mounted on a mouthpiece, leaving a small gap between the reed and the edge of the mouthpiece. The player blows against the reed, causing it to vibrate, which opens and closes the air chamber. This causes pulsations in the column of air, which in turn creates the instrument's tone.

Clarinets seem to have arisen from a family of earlier single-reed instruments known as chalumeau. There is no existing repertory for the chalumeau, and it is unclear exactly how these instruments differed from early clarinets. The Denner family of Nuremberg is credited with creating the first clarinets, around the turn of the 18th century. They added a "speaker key," enabling the clarinet to play in the higher register (the earlier chalumeau was limited to one octave). Eventually, more keys were added, further extending the instrument's range. The most important innovation came in 1842, when French clarinetist Hyacinth Klosé (1808–1880) introduced the Boehm fingering system to the clarinet, making it easier to play in tune in all the keys. Metal and wooden clarinets were made throughout the 19th century, some with modern fingering, some with the older style. The construction of the instrument wasn't standardized until the early years of the 20th century.

Clarinets are reported in various orchestral ensembles in Germany, France, and England from the 1730s on, but were still unknown in many parts of Europe. Mozart did much to champion the instrument, writing a clarinet concerto and a quintet for clarinet and strings. In 1778, he wrote to his father lamenting the fact that clarinets were not yet a part of the orchestra: "Oh, if only we had clarinets; you can't guess the lordly effect of a symphony with flutes, oboes, and clarinets." His "Paris" symphony, composed in the same year, is scored to include clarinets.

Like the oboe, the clarinet was made in many different sizes and styles, but none of these variants worked their way into the modern orchestra.

Recommended Listening

Alan Hacker performs on clarinets from the Baroque, Classical, and Romantic eras on *The Clarinet Collection* (Amon Ra SAR CD-10), with works by D. Scarlatti, Telemann, Handel, Mozart, Schumann, Verdi, and others. Accompaniment is provided by a variety of period keyboards.

THE TRUMPET

The trumpet is the instrument that has undergone the greatest transformation over the last 400 years. Most of the classical composers did not use it to any great extent, except for special effects, because the trumpets at their disposal were fairly limited. It wasn't until the mid-19th century, with the introduction of valved trumpets, that the instrument achieved any great sophistication. And, because of its background, it remained primarily a military and popular band instrument rather than an orchestral one.

Early trumpets were "natural horns." They did not have any valves or extra tubing, so they could only play one note and its fundamentals. If you've studied acoustics, you know that a vibrating column of air (or a string) produces a fundamental tone; this is a note that is strongly heard when you blow into a simple horn. But the vibrating air also produces partials, or smaller subdivisions of the primary tone. Thus, a bugle player can, by exciting these partials, play taps or reveille, and so players of simple trumpets could play several different notes.

To overcome this limitation, orchestras in Bach's time, if they had the wherewithal, would equip their trumpeters with several instruments, each pitched to a different key. In this way, the trumpeter could use the appropriate instrument to play the notes called for in the score. As you get higher and higher in pitch, the partials fall closer and closer together. Eighteenth-century composers took advantage of this trick of nature to compose elaborate high-pitched flourishes to be performed on the trumpet; a famous example can be heard in Bach's Brandenburg Concerto No. 2 in F Major.

In the mid-18th century, extra lengths of tubing, or crooks, were introduced. By adding these to the trumpet, the player could play in different keys; when the air column is made longer, the fundamental pitch of the instrument is lowered. Different lengths of tubing could thus be added for different fundamental tones. Taking these crooks on and off was not a simple procedure, so the composer had to allow for the trumpeter to make the adjustment necessary to play in another key. Most orchestras had at least two trumpets for the trumpeter to give him some flexibility.

Finally, a group of designers working on the trumpet introduced a true valve system. Here the trumpet is equipped with extra tubing that is opened and closed by different valves controlled by keys. In this way, the trumpeter can easily lengthen or shorten the air column, thereby allowing him to play all the notes of the scale as either fundamentals or partials.

Surprisingly, the trumpet fell out of favor after the Baroque era, and is rarely heard in the orchestral works of Mozart, Haydn, or Beethoven, except for special effect. Rather than using the flexible upper register of the instrument, these composers tended to use the fundamental pitches and a few low-pitched partials. The instrument was used for accent or emphasis, almost percussively, rather than melodically as it had been used by Bach.

Recommended Listening

Baroque Trumpet Music (Deutsche Harmonia Mundi 77027-2-RC) presents works by Bach, Handel, Telemann, and others performed on period instruments. *Greatest Hits of the Trumpet* (Columbia Masterworks MLK-45525) is a silly title but a good collection of twenty-six works for trumpet and orchestra by Bach, Berlioz, Copland, Handel, Stravinsky, Strauss, Haydn, and others. John Wallace has recorded a number of CDs of Baroque trumpet music of different countries, including *Rule Britannia* (Nimbus NI-5155), *Trumpet Music from the Italian Baroque* (Nimbus NI-5079), and

T for Trumpeter (Nimbus NI-5065), a collection of concerti and fanfares by C. M. von Weber, Hummel, F. D. Weber, Altenburg, and others.

The Orchestra

When you think of an orchestra today, you probably picture a conductor in tails standing on a podium facing a large ensemble, with the instruments divided into defined sections, each with its own particular role to play. In fact, this conception of an orchestra is relatively new, having come about only over the last century and a half. Prior to that, the orchestra was quite a different beast.

Originally, composers had to write for whatever ensemble was available to them. If a duke or king had violins, violas, cellos, a flute, and a trumpet, then the music would be scored for those instruments! This was not an artistic choice, but merely a practical one. The first "orchestras" were no more than large collections of instrumentalists gathered by a nobleman to impress his peers. Thus, Louis XIV had his famous "vingt-quatre violins du roi" (twenty-four violins of the king), a group maintained primarily for ceremonial occasions that so impressed King Charles II of England that he vowed to have a larger and more impressive ensemble of his own!

In the 18th century, the orchestra began to become more defined, although it still could consist of a variety of instruments. A central player in the orchestra was the harpsichordist or keyboardist; he served as a kind of conductor, playing a constant bass accompaniment to the entire work and signaling when different instruments should play. The "figured bass," as it was called, was a sketched-in accompaniment part; the composer merely indicated the key harmonic note, and the harpsichordist was expected to improvise an appropriate harmony freely around it. This was made easier by the fact that the composer often took the keyboardist's role.

The various instrumental roles in the early orchestra were not clearly defined. In other words, flutes were as likely to play the main melody as violins, although the strings did tend to take the lead. The strings usually were used throughout a composition, but the supporting winds would come and go—flute in one part, clarinet in another, for example. The reason is simple: the band probably featured doubling, and sometimes trebling, of instruments, so the clarinetist might also play oboe and flute and couldn't be expected to play all three at once!

One of the most influential orchestras of this period was led by Johann W. A. Stamitz (1717–1757) in Mannheim, Germany. Stamitz was revolutionary in introducing new instruments to the orchestral ensemble, including the clarinet and flute. But the key ingredient in his success was the fact that he rehearsed his orchestra vigorously, and this discipline showed in their performances. He also introduced several modern effects to the orchestra, including crescendo (or the gradual increasing in volume from soft to loud). Earlier orchestras would stop abruptly after playing a soft passage and then, after an awkward silence, go full force to a loud one!

By the early 19th century, the "modern" orchestra was just coming into being. Innovations in musical instrument construction, as described throughout this chapter, made for changes in the makeup of the orchestra. The harpsichord playing its "figured bass" was gradually removed. The violins came to the fore as the lead instruments; the first violinist, or concertmaster, even took over the conducting responsibilities that the harpsichord player had previously held. However, by the mid-19th century, a formal "conductor" was introduced, with the job of managing the orchestra.

Beethoven's great symphonic compositions could not have been written without the newly improved orchestra. But, on the other hand, the demands of Beethoven's great writing, and his imaginative use of the instruments at his disposal, led to a maturing of the orchestra. The instrumental makeup called for in Beethoven's first symphony (1800) became a standard for Romantic orchestras: violins (divided into first and second), violas, cellos, and double basses; two flutes, oboes, clarinets, bassoons, trumpets, and horns; and kettledrums.

The 19th-century orchestra was also unique in that it was not supported by a royal court. Instead, civic organizations took on the task of raising the funds to maintain and operate their own orchestras. In 1842, New York City founded a "Philharmonic Society" to form an orchestra, which continues to this day as the New York Philharmonic Orchestra. Vienna acted in the same year to establish the Vienna Philharmonic Orchestra, so that both orchestras celebrated their 150th year of continuous operation in 1992. Other cities in the U.S. and Europe followed suit, until today there is hardly a major metropolitan center that lacks an orchestra.

Classical Music for Unusual Musical Instruments

The instruments profiled in this chapter represent those that have survived as the major players in today's classical ensembles. But there were many other instruments that were at one time or another part of the classical scene, attracting the attention of composers major and minor. A few of these lesser-known instruments are:

Glass Harmonica: Perfected by American amateur scientist Benjamin Franklin, the glass harmonica consists of glasses filled with different amounts of water. When the player rubs a moistened finger around the edge of the glass, a shimmering tone is produced (undoubtedly you have tried this yourself on a crystal wine glass). Mozart played the instrument at age seventeen and composed for it, and both Haydn and Beethoven wrote solos for it. The instrument may be heard on *Music for Glass Harmonica* (Vox Unique VU 9008), in solo and ensemble settings.

Mandolin: Today we associate this instrument, tuned like a violin with four sets of paired strings, with country and bluegrass music. But earlier forms of the instrument were well known in Italy and Germany. Vivaldi wrote several concerti for mandolin and orchestra (one of which was featured in the film *Kramer vs. Kramer*), and Beethoven wrote at least five pieces for mandolin and piano. Recordings of Vivaldi's mandolin concerti include: *Concerto in C for Mandolin and Orchestra* (Deutsche Grammophon 413664-4 GMF), *Concerto in G for 2 Mandolins and Orchestra* (Deutsche Grammophon ARC-415674-2), and *Concerti for Mandolin and Strings* (Philips 412624-2 PH).

Tambourine: A tambourine craze swept England about the turn of the 19th century, with many young ladies taking up the instrument as an accompaniment to a pianist. Jumping on the bandwagon, Clementi wrote twelve waltzes for piano and tambourine and triangle.

Reed Organ: The reed organ was quite popular in 19th-century Europe and

America. Featuring reeds similar to those found in a harmonica (although larger), the instrument creates music through air pressure driven by manual pedals, which is forced through the individual reeds, causing them to vibrate. Dvořák, Franck, and Reger all composed for it.

Saxophone: When the saxophone was first introduced in the mid-19th century, it was primarily used as a band instrument. However, classical composers were attracted to it; Debussy, Strauss, Bizet, Saint-Saëns, and Delibes all wrote for the saxophone. Debussy's Rhapsody for Saxophone and Orchestra can be heard on Pearl GEMM CD 9348.

Guitar: Most classical music that you hear on guitar is music that was "arranged" for the instrument, drawn either from the Renaissance lute repertory or from the general classical repertory. However, many composers enjoyed playing the guitar as a pastime. Schubert was said to play the instrument in bed each morning upon waking, and Berlioz was also an able guitarist.

English Concertina: Originally found in many ballet and theater orchestras, this relative of the accordion was a popular instrument in mid-19th-century England. Nearly forgotten composers such as Molique and MacFarren wrote concerti for it, and many others wrote original music or arranged popular classical melodies for the instrument.

FOUR
BAROQUE MUSIC

The Baroque period is important for many musical innovations. It was the time in Italy when the first great violinists flourished, composing innovative works including solo sonatas and compositions for violin and orchestra. The Italians also pioneered the concerto grosso form, an important development in the composing of music for larger ensembles. On the Continent, pioneering keyboardists—Couperin and Scarlatti on harpsichord, Buxtehude and Sweelinck on organ—were heard. Keyboard fugues, particularly for the organ, achieved new heights of complexity in the hands of these composer/performers.

In the Baroque era, the line between composer and performer was a thin one. In fact, almost all performing musicians composed music. For this reason, composers tended to specialize: violinists primarily wrote for strings, organists for keyboards, and so on. Or, a composer might choose a single form, such as the concerto grosso, and specialize in that area. It was the rare composer who had wide-enough experience to write in a variety of forms or for different instruments, such as Vivaldi did. And still, Vivaldi was primarily famous as a performer, not as a composer.

Musical prowess tended to run in families. Just as bricklayers might teach their offspring their craft, so organists or violinists would teach their children the family business. Occasionally, a particularly talented family, such as the Bachs of Germany or the Couperins of France, would produce many generations of exceptionally talented musicians who left their mark on the history of Western music. Other families plodded along producing yeoman musicians, with an occasional brighter light appearing from time to time on the musical firmament.

Baroque music is immediately recognizable—and easily parodied—because of its surface brilliance. The Baroques emphasized melodic ornamentation and virtuosic improvisation over harmonic subtleties. Taken to an extreme, the Baroque style can be highly excessive; the word "baroque" has taken on a negative connotation in some art forms, coming to mean overly decorated or tastelessly ornate. But in the hands of the greatest composers, the Baroque style allowed for full musical expression. The techniques that Baroque musicians developed revolutionized the way music was performed. Without this increase in sophistication on the part of musicians and composers alike, the Classical period that came just after the Baroque years would undoubtedly have been delayed.

The Violin Revolution

A small group of Italian musicians and instrument builders helped bring the violin to prominence in the 17th and 18th centuries. Leading this group was Arcangelo Corelli, who paved the way for the greatest and most colorful of the Italian Baroque fiddlers, Antonio Vivaldi.

ARCANGELO CORELLI

b. 1653, Bologna, Italy
d. 1713, Rome, Italy
Corelli was a child prodigy violinist who, by the age of thirteen, was studying violin in Bologna and, just four years later, was elected to that city's prestigious Academia Filarmonica. Soon af-

ter, he moved to Rome, where he spent his life performing on the violin, composing, and leading musical ensembles.

Corelli is known as the "father" of the concerto grosso (which literally means "big concerto"). A concerto alternates solo and orchestral parts: a soloist, such as a violinist, plays a melody, then the orchestra responds, and then the soloist plays again, and so on. In the concerto grosso, the entire orchestra is divided into two parts: the concertino, usually two solo violins and accompanying cello and harpsichord, and the ripieno, the entire orchestra. The concertino takes the part of the "soloist," playing a section, and then the orchestra or ripieno responds. This dramatic interplay between voices of the orchestra was entirely new and impressive to listeners in Corelli's day. It foreshadowed the less-mechanical use of orchestral voices in later Classical and Romantic works.

Corelli was a difficult taskmaster as an orchestral leader, demanding strict precision from his musicians. Charles Burney, a famous British musicologist, observed Corelli at work and commented on how he demanded that the violin section play as if it were one voice: "Corelli regarded it as essential . . . that [the violinists'] bowings should all move exactly together, all up or down. . . . He would immediately stop the band if he discovered one irregular bow."

Recommended Listening

Corelli's most important works in his day were his concerti grossi and sonatas for violin and continuo (harpsichord accompaniment). The sonatas, first published in 1700, were staples of the European repertoire for more than 100 years, and helped introduce the new Italian violin techniques to musicians and their audience.

Corelli's *Complete Works* (Europa Musica 350 202) are available on a nine-CD set (priced as five CDs), performed by the Academia Bizantia under the direction of Carlo Chiarappa. His complete concerti grossi are available on the budget-priced Vox Box CDX 5023, consisting of two CDs performed by the Southwest German Chamber Orchestra. The Locatelli Trio has recorded the twelve violin sonatas on two CDs on Hyperion CDA 66381/82, which also features a thirteenth sonata, a reworking of one of Corelli's works by Francesco Geminiani. The trio recording adds cello as a further accompanying instrument to the violin and harpsichord or organ arrangements that would have been heard in Corelli's day. Corelli's trio sonatas of 1689 for two violins and cello, accompanied by theorbo (bass lute) and organ, can be heard on period instruments on Smithsonian Collection ND 035; a different selection can be heard performed by Trevor Pinnock and the well-known English Concert on Deutsche Grammophon ARC-419614-2 AH.

ANTONIO VIVALDI

b. 1678, Venice, Italy
d. 1741, Vienna, Austria

Antonio Vivaldi is best remembered today as the composer of "The Four Seasons," perhaps the best-loved of all classical concerti. But he was quite a prolific composer, writing some 400 other concerti, mostly for violin and orchestra, but also for bassoon, mandolin, guitar, recorder, oboe, and cello, not to mention some 300 other works both religious and secular. Both revered and reviled in his lifetime, Vivaldi's work was influential on both his contemporaries and the composers who followed him. Bach copied many of Vivaldi's concerti by hand, hoping to unravel their mystery. He recognized, as many of his contemporaries did not, that Vivaldi was a master of the concerto form.

Vivaldi's father was a barber/violinist who taught his son the basics of music. Ordained as a priest in 1703, the twenty-five-year-old Vivaldi was hired as a composer and teacher for a girls' orphanage (the Ospedale della Pieta) in Venice. The young orphans who were trained there were highly regarded by noblemen who often chose a wife from within the orphanage's walls. Some of the orphans went on to become well-known musicians in their own right. Vivaldi taught violin, organ, and harpsichord for thirty-seven years at the orphanage, enjoying a rare (for a musician) period of financial stability. Moreover, he could use the house orchestra to hone his compositions.

There are records indicating that Vivaldi traveled throughout Europe during this period, performing his own works and spreading the gospel of the new violin technique. In 1740 he settled in Vienna, hoping to gain employment as a court composer to Charles VI. Apparently after failing to win the nobleman's favor, Vivaldi died penniless.

Although he was a priest, Vivaldi was not exactly pious. Nicknamed "the Red-Headed Priest" because of his fiery temperament, Vivaldi was both a passionate violinist and an unconventional man. He lived openly with his mistress, opera star Anna Giro, for whom he composed many vocal works. His showmanship as a performer did not go unnoticed by his contemporaries. Although lauded as a virtuoso, Vivaldi was criticized for focusing on skill rather than feeling.

Vivaldi was one of the first composers to specify different bowing techniques for the solo strings. He was himself a master of the bow, creating many unusual effects by varying pressure and attack. He also was known to play far up the fingerboard, and may even have had a special violin made with an extralong neck to facilitate playing superhigh notes. One contemporary critic marveled at his technique: "He placed his fingers but a hair's breadth from the bridge so that there was hardly room for the bow. He played thus on all four strings . . . at unbelievable speed." However, the critic added a typical disparaging comment to his review: "I cannot say that it captivated me, because it was more skillfully executed than pleasing to hear."

Vivaldi's music has often been critiqued for being "all flash," virtuosic but soulless. Others have criticized the composer for repeating himself; it is sometimes jokingly said that he did not compose 400 concerti, but rather wrote one concerto 400 times! This is a particularly unfair knock, since many Baroque composers reworked their material. After all, Vivaldi was a working musician who had to produce a great deal of music on short notice. Although much of his music lapsed into obscurity after his death, the revival of Baroque music after World War II brought renewed interest in this great composer. In the 1950 *Schwann* catalog, there were only two recordings of "The Four Seasons" listed; today there are eighty-four, and several more pages of Vivaldi's other works.

Recommended Listening

"The Four Seasons" is one of the most-recorded works in the classical repertoire. In these four concerti, the composer portrays the varying personalities of the four seasons of the year. Each concerto is accompanied by a sonnet written by the composer, and these poems serve as programs for the music, in which the poetic images are echoed. For example, the opening section of the "Spring" concerto features the solo violinist playing passages that echo the calls of birds; these first notes parallel lines in the poem describing the first bird songs of spring. For the budget-minded, RCA Silver Seal 60542-2-RV is a good buy, featuring Salvatore Accardo as the solo violinist with the Orchestra da Camerata Italiana. It also features additional Vivaldi violin concerti. For those who prefer to hear their Baroque music on period instruments, Christopher Hogwood leads the Academy of Ancient Music on Oiseau 410126-2 OH. Finally, a good contemporary reading is given by Itzhak Perlman with the Israel Philharmonic led by Zubin Mehta on Deutsche Grammophon 419214-2 GH.

If you enjoy "The Four Seasons," why not explore Vivaldi's other violin concerti? Some good places to begin include the Aulos Ensemble's performance on period instruments of the Violin Concerto in D Major, along with cello, oboe, and flute concerti. This two-CD set is issued on Musicmasters 7020-2-C. Trevor Pinnock and the English Concert perform a number of concerti on period instruments, including the violin concerto known as "L'amoroso," or "the beloved," and concerti for bassoon, flute, oboe, viola d'amore and lute, and two violins (Deutsche Grammophon ARC-419615-2 AH). For interpretations on modern instruments, Herbert von Karajan and the Berlin Philharmonic perform two violin concerti, plus a concerto for two violins and orchestra, and a flute concerto on Deutsche Grammophon 423226-2 GMW.

Vivaldi wrote many concerti for different instruments, among the most charming of which are his mandolin concerti. Be careful when purchasing recordings of these works, because some substitute guitar for mandolin, a totally inappropriate change. Try Forlane UCD-16548, which features the Concerti for Mandolin and Strings in C Major and D Major, plus the Concerto in G Major for Two Mandolins and Strings and the Concerto in C Major for Two Mandolins and Orchestra, plus a selection of Vivaldi's oboe concerti. For recorder fans, there are several charming concerti. Several of the better-known works have been recorded by the Academy of Saint Martin-in-the-Fields on Philips 412874-2 PH.

For those who want an overview of this composer's works, there is *Vivaldi's Greatest Hits* (Columbia Masterworks MLK-45810), featuring selections from "The Four Seasons," the Mandolin Concerto in C Major, the Double-mandolin Concerto in G Major, the Guitar Concerto in D Major, and other works performed by the New York Philharmonic, the English Chamber Orchestra, the Boston Pops, and other artists. Pro Arte has also issued a CD called *Vivaldi's Greatest Hits* (CDM-816), featuring "The Four Seasons" excerpts plus the Bassoon Concerto in E Major, the Oboe Concerto in F Major, and other works.

GIUSEPPE TARTINI

b. 1692, Pirano, Italy
d. 1770, Padua, Italy

Tartini's life story reads like a gothic romance or the plot of an Italian opera! It could only have unfolded in 18th-century Italy. Born to a wealthy family, Tartini traveled to Padua to study at the age of sixteen. Tartini trained, in turn, for careers in the church, the law, and the army, but discovered his true vocations in fencing and fiddling. When he was eighteen, he secretly married a young girl who was the ward of a Paduan priest, against the wishes of the powerful clergyman. Tartini fled town to escape the priest's wrath, hiding out in a monastery in Assisi for three years.

At the monastery, he met a musician nicknamed "the Bohemian Priest," a passionate violinist who greatly influenced the young musician. Tartini made several important discoveries while studying music at the monastery. When playing a double-stop, or two strings at once, he discovered that he could hear a third tone, a bass note produced as if by magic. This acoustical phenomenon is known as the "resultant tone." It is still used by violinists today to check the tuning of their instrument; if the two strings are not perfectly in tune, the resultant tone will not be produced.

Tartini made several improvements to the violin bow, lightening it so that it could be more easily manipulated, improving the grip so it would be easier to hold, and changing its overall design. Violin bows at the time resembled hunting bows: they had a very high, pronounced arch. By reducing this arch, Tartini was able to give the violinist greater control over the bow. He also experimented with heavier-gauge strings to improve the tone and volume of his instrument.

Tartini's most famous composition for the violin is a sonata known as the "Devil's Trill." In truly Romantic fashion, Tartini told of how he made a pact with the devil to improve his violin playing: "One night I dreamed that I had made a bargain with the devil for my soul. The idea suggested itself to hand him my violin to see what he would do with it. Great was my astonishment when I heard him play, with consummate skill, a sonata of such exquisite beauty that it surpassed the boldest flights of my imagination. I felt enraptured . . . and—I awoke. Seizing my violin I tried to reproduce the sounds I had heard. But in vain. The piece I then composed, 'The Devil's Sonata,' although the best I ever wrote, how far was it below the one I had heard in my dream!" Stories of the devil teaching music to mortals are a part of world folklore, and undoubtedly Tartini used this one as a means of promoting his new composition. The violin techniques he introduced were so breathtaking to his contemporaries, however, that they may well have believed that they had supernatural origins.

Tartini's exile ended when his identity was exposed one day while he was playing violin during a church service. His musical talents led the Paduan priest to forgive him, and he was able to return to Padua and a life as a performer, composer, and teacher.

Recommended Listening

There is no CD issue currently available of the "Devil's Trill." One unaccompanied sonata, Sonata No. 13, is available on Fone

83F 01, along with works by Bartók, Kreisler, Schubert, and other more recent composers. Another with keyboard continuo, the Sonata in G Minor, is available on Pavane ADW 7220, along with works by Mozart and Schubert.

FRANCESCO GEMINIANI

b. circa 1687, Lucca, Italy
d. 1762, Dublin, Ireland

Geminiani, a student of Corelli's, was one of the most widely traveled of all the Italians, finally settling in London and Dublin at the far western end of Europe. His compositions are models of the Baroque style, with intricately ornamented melodies and a complex interweaving of parts in his ensemble works.

Performing in his hometown of Lucca from 1707 to 1710, Geminiani was nicknamed "Il Furibondo" (the wild or furious one) by his contemporary Tartini. A great soloist, Geminiani's untamed style and elaborate variations made it almost impossible for him to perform in an ensemble.

Geminiani's fame came when he settled in England. Being so far removed from the musical innovations of the Continent, the English were amazed to hear the Corelli-influenced style of this young soloist. Geminiani not only played brilliantly, he played differently. He held the violin under his chin on the left side of the tailpiece. Many English players were still holding the violin upright; others were following the Continental style of holding it under the chin on the right side of the tailpiece, an awkward position that made it more difficult to finger up the neck. Geminiani is also said to have introduced the symbols for crescendo (gradually increase volume) and decrescendo (gradually decrease volume) in music, so we must suppose that he used these subtle changes in volume in his own playing.

Geminiani's violin instruction book, *Art of Playing the Violin*, published in 1751, codified the new Italian style for the next generation of players. It introduced elements of technique that revolutionized violin playing, such as how to handle the bow, fret the strings, and hold the instrument. It also preached Geminiani's uniquely individualistic theories of performance. The great violinist does not slavishly follow the score, he said, but adds his own personal touch to playing, including expressive trills, variations, shakes, and changes in tone, volume, and attack.

Recommended Listening

Editio Classica 77010-2-RG is the only currently available CD of Geminiani's violin concerti, performed by La Petite Bande. *The Art of Playing Guitar*, a series of eleven sonatas composed in 1760 for guitar, cello, and harpsichord, is available on White Label HRC-046, along with Vivaldi's guitar and mandolin concerti.

Masters of the Keyboards

The Baroque period not only ushered in a new age for the violin, it also saw a revolution in the playing of keyboard instruments. Innovations in the design and manufacture of these instruments contributed to the growth in their popularity, but it took great composer/performers to write new music to exploit these improvements. We'll look at the achievements of four of these keyboard virtuosi who influenced both the music of the age and the players who followed them.

JAN PIETERSZOON SWEELINCK

b. 1562, Amsterdam, Netherlands
d. 1621, Amsterdam, Netherlands
Sweelinck was one of the first great organists, born and bred to the instrument. His father was organist at the Old Church in Amsterdam. Jan followed him in this prestigious post, and Jan's son took the seat after his death, making the Sweelincks the house organists at this church for over a century. Sweelinck cut a grand figure in Amsterdam, and many society swells came to church just to hear him play. One contemporary said: "There was a wonderful concourse every day [he played]; every one was proud to have known, seen, heard the man." The townsfolk were so proud of him that they purchased a "clavicembalo," an Italian form of

the harpsichord, for him to use, and he traveled throughout Holland playing the instrument. Sweelinck's playing was widely admired, and students came from Germany, Sweden, and farther afield in Europe to learn his style. His influence on German organists was felt over a century after his death in the playing of Bach.

Sweelinck was one of the first organists to take advantage of the newly introduced pedalboard for the feet, writing independent melodic parts to be played on the pedals. He also developed some of the earliest fugues for the organ. He was very much influenced by two English organists resident in central Europe at the time: John Bull, who played in Antwerp, and Peter Philips, who was employed in Brussels. Sweelinck wrote a treatise on composing for the organ, using as an example a canon written by Bull. Bull returned the favor by writing a fantasia on a theme by Sweelinck.

Recommended Listening

Four of Sweelinck's organ works can be heard performed by Piet Kee on Chandos CHAN 0514, along with select works by Dietrich Buxtehude. Gustav Leonhardt plays a wider selection of Sweelinck's organ works on Editio Classica 77148-2-RG. His "Fantasia Chromatica" for harpsichord, performed by J. E. Dähler, is featured on Claves CD 50-511, along with later works by Bach, Haydn, Mozart, Byrd, and Schubert, showing how the style of composition and performance for harpsichord changed over several hundred years.

DIETRICH BUXTEHUDE

b. 1637, Helsingborg, Denmark
d. 1707, Lübeck, Germany

Buxtehude was a master organist and composer of church music for the instrument. There is some argument concerning his place of birth: the composer gave his nationality as Danish, although some believe he was a German or a Swede. His father was a church organist for thirty-two years and undoubtedly trained his son in the craft. At age thirty-one, Buxtehude landed one of the most lucrative and important positions in the German church as organist at Lübeck. He was determined to make the church a center of musical activity, going beyond his organ-playing duties to found a concert series of religious-oriented chamber music held for five weekends before Christmas. The fame of this series led the young Bach to make a 200-mile pilgrimage to hear Buxtehude play and eventually to study with the master.

Buxtehude was one of the first great composers of fugues for the organ. He used the pedals to provide a bass voice in his fugues, and was probably the first organ composer to conceive of fugal themes with the capabilities of the instrument in mind. Although he composed chorales (music based on hymns), he is best remembered for his "free" organ works, drawing on his own melodic inspiration. His compositions feature ornate improvisation, and also call for crossing of the hands, which was a relatively new technique that allowed the organist to play more freely in the upper registers. However, it is said that in old age Buxtehude had become so portly that he could no longer cross his left hand over his right! His ornately crafted compositions influenced the young Bach, and he is chiefly remembered today for the inspiration he provided the younger and greater composer.

Recommended Listening

Buxtehude's complete organ works have been recorded by Wolfgang Rübsam for Bellaphon on nine CDs, with Volumes 4 and 7 not yet available (690.01.007, 017, 023, 028, 029, 034, 035). For a less encyclopedic introduction to Buxtehude's organ works, try Virgin Classics VC 7 91139-2 for a collection of chorales, preludes, toccatas, and a passacaglia performed by Nicholas Danby.

Who the H--- was Pachelbel?

One of the most popular classical compositions is Pachelbel's Kanon in D Major. Originally composed for organ, it is available in various arrangements, including a Boston Pops orchestral arrangement and arrangements for brass quintet, various early-instrument ensembles, and harp ensemble. RCA has gone so far as to issue an entire CD devoted to different interpretations of this work: *Pachelbel's Greatest Hit* (RCA Gold Seal 60712-2-RG). A favorite at weddings, the piece was featured in the Oscar-winning motion picture *Ordinary*

People, and the Musical Heritage Society claims it is one of their best-selling works.

Johann Pachelbel (1653–1706) was a German church organist born in Nuremberg and active in Vienna, Eisenach, and Stuttgart. His works were highly influential on his contemporaries, including Bach, and he fathered two organists, Wilhelm Hieronymus (c. 1685–1764) and Carl Theodore (1690–1750). Carl strayed far from home, coming to the New World in the 1740s, working in Boston, Newport, Rhode Island, and finally settling in Charleston, South Carolina. He must have been one of the first active German organists in this country, although we can't be sure if he brought his father's "big hit" with him to the New World!

FRANÇOIS COUPERIN

b. 1668, Paris, France

d. 1733, Paris, France

The Couperin family was active on the French music scene for more than two centuries. The earliest musical Couperin we know of was born in 1626, and the last died around the middle of the 19th century, with nine different Couperins serving as organist at the Church of St. Gervais in Paris at one time or another. The family was notable for its talented male and female musicians. Some Couperins were organ, harpsichord, violin, or viola players, some were renowned as vocalists, and others gained their laurels by composing. François Couperin, the most famous of all of the musical family, was nicknamed "Couperin le Grand" (The Great Couperin) because of his unusual achievements.

Couperin began his musical career at the top, working as private organist at King Louis XIV's chapel at Versailles at the age of twenty-five. Three years later, he gained additional employment at St. Gervais, the chapel that would be home to so many Couperins. In 1717, he was appointed harpsichordist to King Louis XV, a position he held until three years before his death. His daughter, another talented player, took over when he became too ill to play and was the first woman to hold this coveted position.

Couperin is remembered today for his many compositions for the harpsichord. These short pieces took the form of portraits of well-known people, imitations of nature, sketches of feelings, or imitations of sounds or motion, such as bagpipes or windmills. Couperin's work was among the first great "program music" (program music is written to illustrate a specific subject). These many short works were often gathered into suites, the most famous being the "Annals of the Great and Ancient Minstrelsy," which celebrated the settlement of a dispute among Parisian musicians in 1707. Each section of the "Annals" had a descriptive title (such as the final section, "Rout of the Whole Troupe, Caused by the Drunkards, Bears, and Monkeys") and all in all gave a fanciful picture of the musical life of early 18th-century France. Couperin also gathered four books of his harpsichord works for publication in his lifetime; these appeared in 1713, 1716, 1722, and 1730 and were influential on harpsichordists throughout Europe.

In addition to his harpsichord music, Couperin wrote for the organ, religious vocal music, songs, and works for chamber orchestra. Couperin also wrote an influential instruction book for harpsichord, *L'art de toucher le clavecin*, which helped spread his composing style and playing techniques throughout Europe. There are many stylistic similarities between Bach's harpsichord music and Couperin's; Bach's harpsichord playing was deeply influenced by the work of the French master.

Recommended Listening

Kenneth Gilbert performs Couperin's four books of harpsichord music on Harmonia Mundi. The first two books consist of two, three-CD sets, HMA-190351/53, 190354/56; the second two books are presented on two two-CD sets, HMA-190357/58 and 190359/60. On *Homage à François Couperin* (Harmonia Mundi HMC-901275), harpsichordist Davitt Moroney presents ten harpsichord pieces by the French composer, paired with pieces by his contemporaries that were influenced by the Couperin pieces.

DOMENICO SCARLATTI

b. 1685, Rome, Italy
d. 1757, Rome, Italy

Scarlatti came from a musical family, with his father Alessandro being a famous composer of operas. Born in the same year as Bach and Handel, and dying within seven years of both, Scarlatti was the first keyboard virtuoso of his age, traveling widely through Europe and spreading new performance techniques. At age twenty-three he had the chance to compete on the keyboards against Handel, who was visiting Rome at the time. Judged equals on the harpsichord, the German edged out the Italian on the organ. They remained lifelong friends.

Typically of composers of the time, Scarlatti was often employed by the church, most notably working as musical director at St. Peter's Basilica in Rome. He also toured extensively throughout Europe as a keyboardist. For the last twenty-eight years of his life he took up permanent residence in Spain, deeply influencing local harpsichord music.

Scarlatti is most famous for his sonatas for the harpsichord, although they are not sonatas in the modern sense. In the 18th century, the term "sonata" was loosely applied to any composition for either a solo instrument or a soloist accompanied by harpsichord (such as violin and harpsichord). Although modern sonatas usually have three contrasting parts, almost all of the 545 keyboard sonatas written by Scarlatti are in a single part; they are more like "studies" than sonatas. Only thirty of these works were published in Scarlatti's lifetime. However, in the 100 years following Scarlatti's death, a number of publishers, primarily in England, found a large market for his works.

Recommended Listening

For those deep of pocket, all of Scarlatti's sonatas for harpsichord and organ are available on thirty-four CDs on Erato 45309-2 (they do give you a price break, giving you thirty-four CDs for the price of twenty!). Trevor Pinnock plays a selection of the harpsichord sonatas on Deutsche Grammophon ARC-419632-2 AH. Scarlatti's sonatas have also been transcribed for piano and guitar. You can hear the great pianist Vladimir Horowitz playing seventeen of the most famous of these works on Columbia Masterworks MK-42410. Guitar versions can be heard on Deutsche Grammophon DG 413783-2 GH, transcribed and performed by Narcisco Yepes.

FIVE

CLASSICAL GIANTS: BACH AND HANDEL

The Classical age "begins" in the year 1685 with the births of Bach and Handel, two of the giants of the era. They are both transitional figures; much of their music shows the strong influence of the Baroque. But still, their achievements taken as an aggregate— the depth and breadth of their compositions, their contribution to music pedagogy, theory, and performance—mark them as giants in the Classical ranks. Along with Haydn and Mozart, their work stands as a culmination of the development of Classical music.

The Classical era is marked by a renewed interest in balance in composition. While the Baroque emphasized surface beauty and ornamentation, the Classical composers strove for a purity of form and content, with the entire effort of the composer going into making a unified, coherent composition. Melody and harmony came to the fore, with less emphasis on the counterpoint so favored by the Baroque composers (although Bach continued to compose great organ fugues, so that these works were a culmination of the best of the Baroque). The Classical composer began to have access to modern musical instruments—the modern violin, piano, and wind instruments—plus worked with modern ensembles—the string quartet and the beginnings of the orchestra.

The Classical composers stood on the cusp of a revolution in the way music was made and supported in Europe. The great courts were beginning to dissolve; revolution was in the air. The church was fragmenting as Protestants questioned the authority of the Pope. So, the two great employers of musicians, church and court, were fading from the scene. Where a Baroque organist might have spent his entire life employed by a single church, he now might have to look elsewhere for support. This meant that composers had to become more versatile. For instance, Bach was not only a great organist and composer of church music. He also worked for a time as an orchestra conductor and ended his career as a choirmaster at a boys' school. Composers in the Classical era began to cater to popular taste; the growth of a monied middle class meant that there was a new, paying audience that was interested in enjoying music. This revolution would be completed by the Romantic composers.

Because the Classical composers were so versatile, we'll spend a little more time looking at their lives and work. To make things easier for you, I've divided their works by type in the recommended-listening sections so you can quickly find the compositions that most interest you.

JOHANN SEBASTIAN BACH

b. 1685, Eisenach, Germany
d. 1750, Leipzig, Germany

To be a Bach was to be a musician. At one time in the early 18th century, some thirty Bachs were actively performing as organists, including nineteen-year-old Johann Sebastian. Bach's parents—who tragically died when the young composer was only nine years old—were both musically talented, as were many of his siblings, including Johann Christoph, who cared for the youngster after their parents' death.

Bach's musical life began at the age of fifteen, when he obtained a position as a choirboy at Lüneberg, some 200 miles north of the family home. As a chorister, Bach received musical training in singing, playing instruments, and composition. He also heard the organ playing of Georg Bohm (1661–1733), a local master whose talent inspired the young musician to study the instrument. Soon, Bach was in demand as an organist on his own. Four years later, he was hired for his first important post, as an organist in the town of Arnstadt. Bach took a one-month leave during his tenure at Arnstadt to study with the aging and renowned organist and composer Dietrich Buxtehude. The month soon mushroomed into three months, with Bach eagerly learning the ornate style of the elder player. The congregation at Arnstadt was somewhat shocked when he returned; the heavily ornamented style of Buxtehude was considered radical by church members who were used to simpler fare.

In 1708, Bach obtained his first long-term employment, as organist at the Ducal Chapel in Weimar. For nine years, Bach enjoyed secure employment and access to an excellent organ. In Weimar he composed his most famous organ works and solidified his position as a master player.

Bach hoped to be promoted to the prestigious position of "kapellmeister," or orchestral director, in Weimar, but, when the position was vacated in 1716, the Duke overlooked Bach. Disappointed by this slight, Bach accepted an offer to be orchestral director in the town of Cöthen in 1717. He spent six years at Cöthen, leading a highly professional orchestra of eighteen musicians and composing much of his famous orchestral music. Additionally, he married for the second time, choosing Anna Magdalena Wülcken, daughter of the town trumpeter, as his bride. Bach's keyboard studies, written to help his wife master the clavier and collected under the name *The Little Clavier Book of Anna Magdalena Bach*, are still used today for the training of pianists.

Bach's success at Cöthen ultimately proved unsatisfying; he missed his work as an organist, and his deep religious feelings made him value composing religious music over secular works. In 1723, he accepted the position of "cantor" or head of the music school at the St. Thomas-schule in Leipzig. He returned to composing religious works, but the long hours and difficult working conditions, coupled with the responsibility of training young and often unruly boys, ultimately reduced Bach's work to drudgery. Still, Bach spent seventeen years in this school, until his death in 1750.

Surprisingly, Bach's work during the later part of his life was little appreciated. His compositions were considered old-fashioned, and he was already being overshadowed by the more modern, Italian-influenced works of two of his sons, Carl Philip Emmanuel and Johann Christian. It would take another 100 years for Bach's work to be rediscovered.

Recommended Listening

Overviews

There are several decent collections that give an introduction to this composer's best-loved works. These include *Bach's Greatest Hits Volumes 1 and 2* (Columbia Masterworks MLK 39431 and 39442), featuring a full roster of Columbia artists, including the Philadelphia Orchestra, E. Power Biggs, the Mormon Tabernacle Choir, Glenn Gould, and synthesizer player Wendy Carlos; *Bach Is Best* (Vox/Turnabout CT-4804X), a budget-priced sampler; and *Bach's Greatest Hits* (Pro Arte CDM-801), featuring various German artists and orchestras.

Orchestral Works

The six Brandenburg concerti are Bach's most famous orchestral works. They are based on the Italian concerto grosso form, but also feature important innovations. In previous Italian works, the concertino, or soloists, usually consisted of two violins and a bass, but Bach expanded the range of soloists to include woodwinds and brass as well as strings. He chose specific solo instruments for each concerto, so that each has its own characteristic sound.

All of the Brandenburgs are written in the standard concerto form of three movements (quick-slow-quick) except the first, which has an additional movement, a minuet, at its conclusion, and the third, which has only two parts (two slowly sounded chords are played between the parts to fill the gap). While many of the earlier Italian concerti grossi were mechanically written, Bach showed how the interplay between soloists and orchestra could become an integral part of the thematic development of each work; the interchange arises from the demands of the music rather than being an arbitrary schema imposed by the composer on his material.

Perhaps the most often performed of the concerti is the fifth, scored for violin, flute, and harpsichord. The first movement features an astonishing harpsichord solo, particularly when you consider that the instrument was usually relegated to a subsidiary position in the orchestra of Bach's time, playing simple arpeggios to accompany the melody. Although the fifth is the most often performed, all six Brandenbergs merit close listening.

A Musical Resume

Have you ever sent a resume and felt that it just ended up in someone's circular file? Bach must have felt similar frustration in 1721, when his employment at Cöthen was suddenly in jeopardy. The Duke had remarried, and his new bride was not musically inclined. Bach needed employment to support his growing family, so he gathered together six of his best concerti composed during his stay at Cöthen and sent them as a kind of "musical resume" to the Margrave of Brandenburg (and perhaps to other noblemen as well). Apparently, no answer was forthcoming, because Bach subsequently was employed in 1723 as a schoolteacher in Leipzig.

Luckily, the Brandenburg concerti did not end up in the circular file, but they did molder in the Brandenburg library until after the composer's death, when these valuable and wonderful pieces of music were rediscovered. Because they were found in Brandenburg, they became known as the "Brandenburg concerti," even though Bach had no connection with that town during his lifetime.

There are so many recordings available of the Brandenburg concerti that it is impossible to select a few as "the best." Pablo Casals's mid-'60s recordings with the Marlboro Festival Orchestra, recently re-issued on two CDs (Sony Classical SMK 46253, 46254), are particularly fine interpretations; Bach's first orchestral suite is also featured on these discs. Deutsche Grammophon has issued Herbert von Karajan's interpretation of these works with the Berlin Philharmonic, also on a two-CD set (DG 431173-2 GGA2). If you are interested in hearing the work on period instruments, you might try the Orchestra of the Age of Enlightenment, on a two-CD set (Virgin Classics VCD 7 90747-2).

The Concerto in D Minor for Two Violins and Orchestra is known as the "Double Concerto," and comes from Bach's Cöthen period. The interplay between the two soloists is quite complex, making it a favorite showpiece for today's virtuosi. Choreographer George Balanchine used this work as the music for his *Concerto Barocco*, further popularizing it.

There are a plethora of recordings of this concerto. Itzhak Perlman and Isaac Stern have recorded the work with the New York Philharmonic under the leadership of Zubin Mehta (Columbia Masterworks MK-36692); it is packaged with works by Vivaldi and Mozart. Pinchas Zukerman and J. L. Garcia recorded the work on RCA Red Seal 60718-2-RC, with Zukerman conducting the English Chamber Orchestra; other violin concerti by Bach are also featured on this package. Jascha Heifetz's historic recording is featured on RCA 6778-2 RC, along with works by Brahms and Mozart.

Bach's orchestral suites, or groupings of popular dance melodies arranged for orchestra, show the strong influence of the French composer Couperin. Their light, airy quality is quite a contrast to Bach's rigorously developed keyboard works. The third suite features the famous "Air for the G-String," probably the best-known of all of Bach's melodies. Vox has issued a budget-priced two-CD set of the complete suites (CDX 5040) featuring the Mainz (Germany) Chamber Orchestra.

Keyboard Works

Bach wrote "The Well-tempered Clavier" to show the advantages of equal temperament, a tuning system for keyboard instruments that allows for playing through a variety of keys without hitting glaringly "bad" notes. In Bach's day, there was no agreement as to a standard tuning system; many organs and harpsichords were tuned to the "mean-tone" system, which made for the awkward situation of having separate keys for D-sharp and E-flat and G-sharp and A-flat. This not only made it difficult for keyboard players to accompany other instruments, the mean-tone system was also limited in range to only a few keys; beyond these limits, players produced discordant and unpleasant notes.

Bach used these forty-eight compositions, in all twenty-four major and minor keys, to show the advantages of equal temperament. It was the popularity of these works and their convincing demonstration of the advantages of equal temperament that helped lead to its final adoption in the 19th century as the standard tuning system for the keyboards.

Although composed for harpsichord, these works are today performed on piano as well. The great Glenn Gould recorded the complete two books on piano on a three-CD set on CBS Masterworks M3K-42266. Kenneth Gilbert's complete set on harpsichord is available on four CDs from Deutsche Grammophon ARC-413439-2 AH4. For an interesting interpretation, try jazz pianist Keith Jarrett's selections on a two-CD set issued as ECM New Series 835246-2, combining a straight classical and "new age"/jazz reading of these works.

Bach composed two famous sets of suites for harpsichord, known today as the "French" and "English" suites. The French suites show the influence of harpsichordist/composer François Couperin and the refinement and grace characteristic of the French composers of the era. No one knows how the more somber English suites were named; the fact that the English were age-old rivals of the French may have led someone to give them this title.

Both sets have been recorded on harpsichord and piano. Christopher Hogwood has recorded the complete French suites on harpsichord on a two-CD set on Oiseau-Lyre 411811-2 OH2. The prolific Glenn Gould has recorded the same works on piano (Columbia Masterworks MK 42267), as well as the English suites on a two-CD set including the Partita in B Minor (M2K-42268). Anthony Curtis has recorded the French and English suites on harpsichord on a three-CD set on Teldec 35776 XD.

Bach's Goldberg Variations were not inspired by the incredible sexual prowess of Nathan and Shirley Goldberg (rim shot!) It seems that the Russian envoy to Saxony was a particular fan of harpsichordist Johann Gottlieb Goldberg. He was also a terrific insomniac, and often asked Goldberg to play soothing music that would help lull him to sleep. The envoy commissioned Bach to write these thirty variations on a stately French sarabande to add to Goldberg's soothing repertoire.

Claudio Arrau recorded a rousing version of the variations, issued on two CDs on RCA Gold Seal 7841-2-RG. Trevor Pinnock has recorded them on harpsichord (Deutsche Grammophon 415130-2 AH). The true aficionado can compare Glenn Gould's 1955 and

1981 piano recordings of the Goldberg Variations by purchasing Columbia Masterworks MYK-38749 (1955 version) and MK-37779. Gould's first recording made his reputation: he gave a fiery, Romantic reading to the works, which up to that time had been interpreted in a dry, academic style.

Bach was best known as an organist in his lifetime, and he wrote prolifically for the instrument, particularly during his employment as an organist in Weimar. Bach was both an innovator and a traditionalist in his organ compositions. He built on the traditions established by past masters, writing in forms that they would have recognized. He is well known for his fugues, but he was equally adept at the chorale-prelude (a free-form style, based on theme and improvisation), the toccata (a blazing showpiece for the organist/composer), the fantasia (a freely improvised work), and the traditional dance forms the chaconne and passacaglia (in which the theme and improvisation are stated in the bass notes of the organ). Many of these works have been arranged for orchestra.

The "Art of the Fugue" is a series of showpieces that Bach wrote to demonstrate the complexities and subtleties of fugal writing. These pieces are available in arrangements for harpsichord, brass quintet, saxophone quintet, orchestra, and organ. A fine harpsichord recording by Davitt Moroney is available on Harmonia Mundi 901169/70, a two-CD set. A good cross section of Bach's organ works is offered by popular organist E. Power Biggs on Columbia Masterworks MK 42643, including the Toccata and Fugue in D Minor, the chorale preludes, the Fantasia in G Major, and other works.

Solo Instrumental Works

Bach's most famous solo instrumental works are the sonatas and partitas that he composed for violin during his employment at Cöthen. These twelve works show the influence of the Italian masters, while at the same time revealing an original approach to composing for this instrument. The best-known of these works is the Partita No. 2 in D Minor, ending with the magnificent chaconne. The unaccompanied violinist plays a series of stately chords followed by thirty-one variations, each revealing another aspect of the instrument's capabilities.

Itzhak Perlman's recording of the complete violin sonatas and partitas is available on Angel CDCB-49483, a two-CD set. Lorna Glover recently recorded the works on a Baroque violin, available on Globe GLO 6002, also a two-CD set.

Bach Around the Block

There have been many unusual interpretations of Bach's works, some more successful than others. Most famous, perhaps, is Walter/Wendy Carlos's series of recordings from the late '60s, beginning with the celebrated album *Switched on Bach* (Columbia Masterworks 7194). This album is a tour de force of synthesizer playing married to the best-loved works of Bach, and introduced many a hippie to the sounds of the great Classical composer. Walter Carlos underwent a sex-change in the '70s to become Wendy Carlos, while continuing her work synthesizing the Bach repertoire on *Switched on Bach Vol. 2* (not yet available on CD) and in synthesized versions of the complete Brandenburg concerti (Columbia Masterworks MK-42308, 42309).

Jazz interpretations of Bach have been plentiful. The Modern Jazz Quartet, one of the founders of "chamber jazz," took Bach themes as a starting point on their brilliant album *Blues on Bach* (sadly not currently available on CD). The Loussier Jazz Trio has issued three CDs of jazz/Bach fusions, the most noteworthy being *Bach to the Future* (Chrysalis F21S-21505). The Swingle Singers give a jazzy vocal performance on *Jazz Sebastian Bach* (Philips 824703-2). Percussionist Brian Slawson has issued *Bach on Wood* (Columbia Masterworks 39704), featuring marimbas, xylophones, and other wooden-keyed melodic and percussive instruments.

GEORGE FRIDERIC HANDEL

b. 1685, Halle, Saxony (Germany)

d. 1759, London, England

Handel was born in the same year as Bach and came from a similar North German, Protestant background. Like Bach, he was a master of late-Baroque/early-Classical composition whose work represented the culmination of contrapuntal writing but also looked ahead to the harmonic, balanced style of Classical composition. However, this is where the similarities end.

Today, Handel is best remembered for the "Messiah," performed at Christmastime throughout the world. Yet, this composer is more than a one-hit wonder; he composed operas, songs, orchestral music, and music for the keyboards. Unlike Bach, who worked at the whim of his patrons, Handel moved freely from patron to patron and also was one of the first musicians to produce works for a popular audience without a noble patron. His oratorios are the first religious works written without church sponsorship. Bach wrote religious music when he was employed by the church, and secular music when he was employed by a nobleman; Handel wrote music as the spirit moved him.

The son of a barber/surgeon, Handel showed remarkable musical capabilities from a young age. He outgrew the talents of the local music instructors by his late teens and traveled to Hamburg in 1703, which was the center of German opera at the time. He was hired as a violinist in the opera orchestra and soon mastered the harpsichord as well. In 1705, Handel composed two operas, the beginning of his remarkable output of compositions.

From 1706 to 1710, he traveled widely through Europe, visiting many Italian centers of musical expression. The Italians were delighted with his skills as a composer and performer and gave him the nickname "Il Sassone" (The Saxon). In Italy Handel met Corelli, the great composer of concerti grossi, a style that the German composer was to make his own. He experienced Italian vocal styles, including performances of operas and oratorios, which were far more developed than their German counterparts. One of the many stories from this era has it that Domenico Scarlatti heard Handel playing the harpsichord at a masked ball in Venice and muttered "This must either be the famous Saxon or the Devil himself!"

Handel landed a plum job in 1710 as kapellmeister to Elector George of Hanover. This position gave him considerable freedom to travel, and soon he made a trip to England, where his operas were an enormous success. In 1712, he made a second "brief" trip to England that lasted the rest of his life! Elector George became King George of England in 1714 after the death of Queen Anne, and his arrival in England assured Handel's position there as a court composer.

Handel helped establish an English institution, the Royal

Academy of Music, which was supported by the king and a group of royal musical amateurs. Handel was its musical director from its beginnings in 1720. His fame rested primarily on the Italian-style operas that he composed, which won great popular acclaim. However, an anti-Handel faction at the Academy decided to burst the composer's balloon by hiring a "real" Italian, named Giovanni Battista Bononcini, to write true Italian operas for the group. The rivalry between the composers was described by satirical poet John Byron as a battle between "Tweedledum and Tweedledee," introducing this expression into the language.

Handel's fame as an operatic composer faded after the success of the English folk opera *The Beggar's Opera* by John Gay in 1728. This work popularized a host of operas with folk themes, and Handel's ornately plotted Baroque operas, sung in Italian, quickly lost their vogue. In 1737, Handel finally abandoned the operatic form.

By a lucky fluke, at about the same time, one of Handel's forgotten early oratorios was revived by a boys' choir in London. The success of this revival pointed the way for Handel's final compositions, the great oratorios "Israel in Egypt" (1738) and the "Messiah" (1742). These oratorios were huge successes; they were sung in English and had a grandeur and depth that previous religious choral works lacked. Handel's background in opera gave him an edge in writing dramatic, compelling music.

Recommended Listening

Overviews

Three collections give a good introduction to Handel's best-loved works: *Handel's Greatest Hits* (Columbia Masterworks MLK-39441), featuring "The Harmonious Blacksmith," "Water Music" (selections), and other works; *Handel's Greatest Hits* (Pro Arte CDM-810), with "Water Music," "Royal Fireworks Music," "Messiah" excerpts, and other works; and *The Heroick Mr. Handel* (Vox/Turnabout PVT-7100), with excerpts from "Royal Fireworks Music," "Water Music," and miscellaneous other works.

Instrumental Works

Handel's greatest concerti grossi are collected as his Opus 6,

consisting of twelve works composed in a single month in 1739. Although derived from the model of Corelli, these works outstrip their Italian forebears in melodic depth, orchestral color, and ingenuous construction. The Handel concerti have a logic all their own, with great melodies charging forward in the quick movements and deeply felt moments of introspection in the contrasting slow movements.

Trevor Pinnock and the English Concert perform these works on period instruments on three Deutsche Grammophon CDs, sold separately as ARC-410897-2-AH, 410898, and 410899. A good budget recording featuring a selection of the concerti (nos. 1, 2, 6, and 11) is available from the Southwest German Chamber Orchestra on Vox/Turnabout PVT 7138.

Handel's most famous orchestral work is the "Water Music," composed to entertain King George during a boat trip down the Thames. A contemporary observer described the trip in these words: "On Wednesday evening about 8, the King took water at Whitehall in an open barge . . . the finest symphonies, composed expressly for this occasion by Mr. Handel [were performed by a group of fifty musicians]: which His Majesty liked so well that he caused it to be played over three times in going and returning."

The original "Water Music" was a suite of twenty pieces. Today, it is usually performed as a group of six works. The original complete work has been recorded by Christopher Hogwood and the Academy of Ancient Music on Oiseau 421476-2 OII and by the Academy of Saint Martin-in-the Fields, led by Sir Neville Marriner, on Angel CDC 49810. The shortened version is available in recordings by Eugene Ormandy and the Philadelphia Orchestra (Columbia Masterworks MLK-39441) and André Previn leading the Pittsburgh Symphony (Philips 411047-2 PH).

Another occasional work Handel composed for King George's entertainment is the "Royal Fireworks Music." These pieces were originally composed to be played outdoors during a fireworks display, so it's not surprising that Handel scored them for the loudest possible instruments, including piercing oboes and bassoons. A recording featuring period instruments has been made by the Cleveland Winds, directed by Frederick Fennell (Telarc CD-80038). Modern interpretations include Pierre Boulez with

the New York Philharmonic on Columbia Masterworks MYK-38480 and Yehudi Menuhin leading the Royal Philharmonic on MCA Classics MCAD-6186. Both of these CDs also include the "Water Music" suite.

Handel's most famous keyboard work is known as "The Harmonious Blacksmith," part of his Harpsichord Suite No. 5 in E Major. A standard in the piano student's repertoire, many stories have grown up about this work. One is that Handel was inspired to compose it during a thunderstorm while taking refuge in a blacksmith's shop. This would be creditable, except that the tune did not earn this nickname until its publication by a British music press in 1822, well after Handel's death. It is said that the neighborhood blacksmith loved the tune, singing it loudly at his work, and the enterprising publisher, hearing his song, gave the work its name. Still another version of the story says that the publisher was himself a blacksmith at one time and gave the work this name because he was often asked to play it. Igor Kipnis can be heard playing "The Harmonious Blacksmith," along with other Handelian favorites, on *The Virtuoso Handel* (Nonesuch 79037-2), a budget-priced sampler of Handel's harpsichord works.

The "Messiah"

Although this book is primarily about instrumental music, we can't discuss Handel's achievements and ignore his best-loved work, the "Messiah." The magnificent overture is one of the best pieces of instrumental music that Handel wrote. After the overture come three vocal sections, telling three parts of the life of Christ: the Annunciation, Crucifixion, and Resurrection. Each section has solo vocal arias, choruses, and instrumental passages. In its entirety, the piece consists of more than fifty separate pieces of music, taking a full two and a half hours to perform! The famous "Hallelujah" chorus comes at the end of the second vocal section (not the end of the entire work, as you might expect), and it, of course, is often performed on its own.

Like many other composers of the day, Handel adapted his "Messiah" to the circumstances of its performance and publication, producing nine different versions in all of the work. Scholars have assembled a "standard" version, but there are still some alternatives on the market. Through the miracle of CD technology, with CD players offering the listener the option of rearranging and selecting different tracks, we now have the ultimate "Messiah," produced by

Nicholas McGegan on French Harmonia Mundi 907050/2 on three CDs. Through following instructions in the accompanying booklet, the listener can reconstruct any one of the nine versions (or make up his or her own). Of course, it is a little misleading to say that you get an "authentic" version, since in one performance Handel may have been working with a full orchestra and in another with just sketchy accompaniment. Also, sadly, this is not the best overall interpretation of the "Messiah" around. Still, it's a fascinating experiment worth investigating.

There are many other recordings available of the "Messiah," both in its entirety and in selections. Eugene Ormandy's recording with the Philadelphia Orchestra and the Mormon Tabernacle Choir (Columbia Masterworks M2K-607) on a two-CD set is a typical modern interpretation of the complete work. Christopher Hogwood and the Academy of Ancient Music present the work on period instruments on Oiseau 411858-2 OH3, a three-CD set; a selection of excerpts from this recording is available on Oiseau 400086-2 OH. Another fine period-instrument recording is John Eliot Gardiner's version (Philips 411 041). Leonard Bernstein and the New York Philharmonic recorded a selection of the most famous excerpts on Columbia Masterworks MYK-38481. The Robert Shaw Chorale has recorded the famous choruses from the work on RCA Victrola 7815-2-RV, a budget-priced collection.

SIX

CLASSICAL GIANTS II: HAYDN AND MOZART

Classical music reached its apex in the works of two composers: Franz Joseph Haydn and Wolfgang Amadeus Mozart. These two revolutionized musical forms as diverse as the symphony, string quartet, and opera. Their work was highly influential on all composers who followed them, and helped define the Classical style. It is an odd twist of fate that the two men knew each other, with Haydn's mastery of form influencing the fiery Mozart and Mozart's great talent and deep passion helping Haydn achieve his greatest work.

FRANZ JOSEPH HAYDN

b. 1732, Rohrau, Austria

d. 1809, Vienna, Austria

Born to poor parents in a village settled primarily by Croatian and Slavic immigrants, the son of a wheelwright (someone who makes and repairs wheels for carriages), Franz Joseph Haydn and his younger brother Johann Michael showed musical talent from an early age. Both went on to become prominent musicians and composers, although the elder brother was definitely the more talented and important of the two.

Franz Joseph's musical training began at the age of six, when he went to live with a relative, Johann Frankh, who, in Haydn's words, gave him "more flogging than food." Frankh was a talented musician, and he gave the boy thorough training on several musical instruments and in vocal music. At age eight, Haydn escaped Frankh's household to become a choirboy in St. Stephen's Church of Vienna.

The life of a choirboy was not an easy one. Although a talented youngster could get thorough training in music (along with religious education, Latin, reading and writing, and mathematics), the living conditions were hard and the performance schedule grueling. The choir director (known as the kapellmeister) was often a frustrated musician who had little sympathy for the plight of his boys. The greatest indignity suffered by the boys was that, once their voices changed at puberty, they were ousted from the choir, losing their food and lodging as well as social position.

Haydn struggled through his late teens as best he could, taking the odd teaching or performing job that came along. At age twenty, he met an Italian singing master, Niccolò Porpora (1686–1766), who hired him as an accompanist. Porpora introduced Haydn to many influential people, including his first patron, and to potential students who might employ him as a music teacher. From the mid-1750s on, Haydn's life was looking up, with steadier and better income coming his way. During the 1750s, Haydn composed his first string quartet and symphony. In 1759, he was hired by Count Ferdinand Maximilian von Morzin as musical director for his palace. Sadly, von Morzin died two years later, leaving the composer without employment again.

Haydn was hired in 1761 by Prince Paul Anton Esterházy, the owner of an estate at Eisenstadt, as his music director. Haydn held this position for twenty-nine years. Although isolated from cosmopolitan musical life, he had at his disposal an excellent orchestra and choir for the performance of musical works. Still, Haydn was viewed as a servant of the prince, just like a gardener or cook. His contract with Esterházy gives a picture of the nobility's attitude toward professional musicians: "Haydn . . . must be temperate, not showing himself overbearing toward his musicians . . . he [must] appear in white stockings and white linen, powdered, and with either a pigtail or a tiewig. . . . He should [abstain] from undue familiarity and from vulgarity in eating, drinking, and conversation." Obviously, the 18th-century noble-man viewed musicians less like creative artists and more as crafts-men, a lower class of people who provided a necessary service but who must be instructed to behave in a manner suitable to their position as servants.

Many composers, if cut off from hearing contemporary music and meeting other musicians, might have been stunted in their creative growth. In fact, living outside of a metropolitan area seems to have agreed with the country-born Haydn. In a famous quote, he said: "Cut off as I was from the world, there was no one to confuse me and torment me and I was forced to become original." With twenty-nine years of steady employment, the composer was able to focus on his creative growth and to explore more fully different musical styles and possibilities. Luckily, his employer was a great music lover, and this undoubtedly aided in his own musical maturity.

In 1781, Haydn's musical path intersected with Mozart's. It was a key meeting in both composers' lives. Mozart was only twenty-five, embarking on his extraordinary musical journey, although already a prodigious composer and performer. Haydn was middle-aged and just reaching the height of his powers. The string quartets that Mozart composed after meeting Haydn show the influence of the elder composer in their more sophisticated organization and use of the individual voices within the quartet. Haydn, on the other hand, was able to produce works of greater emotion and depth after meeting Mozart. The two remained life-long friends after this meeting, and their development as com-posers—and the development of Classical music in general—was hastened by their sharing of musical ideas.

In 1790, Esterházy died, once again leaving Haydn patronless. But, in the new world of music, there were opportunities for com-posers to support themselves by performing for a mass audience. A London-based violinist and entrepreneur named Johann Peter Salomon offered Haydn the unheard-of sum of £1200 to come to England to work. Haydn visited the country twice, in 1790 and 1794, premiering his last twelve symphonies, which won wide critical acclaim and revolutionized the symphonic form.

Haydn is generally known as "the Father of the Symphony."

His early symphonic works were similar to other 18th-century symphonies, being nothing more than an enlargement of the overture. By the 1770s though, Haydn had hit on the four-part organization that would become the standard symphonic form: a fast opening movement with two contrasting themes; a slow movement; a minuet (a dance form that previously appeared in the orchestral suite); and a fast-paced finale. Haydn also introduced fuller instrumentation to the symphony, using a wider variety of woodwinds and horns along with the strings. A prolific worker, Haydn composed 104 numbered symphonies, and three others that are generally credited to him. Of these, the most famous are the six so-called "Paris" symphonies, composed in 1764 for a concert series in the French capital, and the twelve "London" symphonies written for Salomon between 1790 and 1795. There are also several well-known individual symphonies from Haydn's pen, such as the "Surprise" and the "Farewell."

Nicknames

Many classical works have earned nicknames, often given to the pieces by critics, music publishers, or the audience itself after the composer's death. Haydn is perhaps unique in the number of nicknames his symphonies and quartets have earned. Here's a selection of a few and the stories behind them.

The **"Farewell"**: This symphony features a famous effect in the last movement as, one by one, the players drop out of the work, leaving the stage. It is said that Haydn and his peers were trying to drop a none-too-subtle hint to Prince Esterházy that they were eager to leave on a well-earned vacation to Vienna. Apparently, the ploy worked. The piece remains a concert favorite.

The **"Toy"**: This is quite an unusual work, scored for two violins, keyboard, double bass, and an array of children's musical instruments, including toy trumpet, drum, rattle, triangle, and bird whistles. It is said that Haydn saw these instruments at a fair and was so enchanted with them that he decided to compose this piece for his band at Eisenstadt as a lark. It's not actually a "symphony," but rather a series of amusing melodies. Many composers have followed in Haydn's footsteps in composing "toy symphonies," to the point where this is recognized as a separate form by musicologists.

The **"Surprise"**: The "surprise" here is the witty way that Haydn ends the slow movement with a bang, a loud chord that the composer said would "make the ladies jump." Apparently even in the 18th century some people snoozed during classical music concerts! This is one of the "London" symphonies.

The "Miracle": One of the more farfetched stories has attached itself to this work. Supposedly, the English audience rushed forward after the premiere to congratulate the composer. Just as they reached the stage, a chandelier over their seats fell to the floor. Had they not been moved to rush the stage, they would have been crushed!

The quartets also have their nicknames. The five so-called "Sun" quartets are known by this name because the symbol of the sun appeared on the first edition of these works; it was the publisher's trademark. The well-loved "Emperor" quartet was based on the Austrian national anthem, "The Emperor's Hymn," composed by Haydn in 1797. Haydn was thrilled to be asked to write a national anthem for his homeland, which had never had one. The tune is based on an old folksong that he had heard in his youth, and it remained the national anthem until Austria reorganized as a republic after World War I. The "Emperor" quartet features this theme in a series of inventive variations, and it remains one of the composer's most often played works.

Along with his symphonic output, the composer wrote roughly eighty string quartets. He was the first composer to treat the four instrumental voices as individuals, each with its own personality. He regularized the quartet form as something distinct from other instrumental works. Haydn composed some of his most expressive works in this idiom, and his achievements in extending the range of emotions and tone colorings that could be achieved in the quartet influenced every composer who came after him, particularly Mozart.

Haydn's last great achievement was the oratorio "The Creation," based on a text written for Handel but rejected by that composer. The work was written without church backing, although Haydn used it to express his deepest religious feelings. The orchestral introduction is a brilliant musical description of the creation of the world out of chaos. Haydn's masterful use of the orchestral voices, colorings, and textures, and his manipulation of dynamics, forecast the work of the great symphonists, such as

Beethoven and Mahler, and the tone poems of the 19th-century Romantics.

Recommended Listening

Orchestral Works

The "Farewell" symphony can be heard on period instruments by Trevor Pinnock and the English Concert (Deutsche Grammophon 429757-2 AH) as part of what Pinnock calls Haydn's "Sturm & Drang" Symphonies (they are released under this title on a series of CDs).

The "Paris" symphonies have been issued on two CDs by the Southwest German Chamber Orchestra conducted by Günther Wich on Intercord INTO 820.772 and 820.773.

The "London" symphonies have been issued as a five-CD set by Herbert von Karajan and the Berlin Philharmonic Orchestra (Deutsche Grammophon 42865702 GSE5) and are also available individually on various recordings. The "Surprise" symphony is available in an interpretation by the Cleveland Orchestra led by George Szell on Sony Classical SBK 46332. The Symphony No. 104 in D Major (the seventh in the series of "London" symphonies which, for some reason, is popularly known as the "London" symphony) is available on a recording by Christopher Hogwood and the Academy of Ancient Music (Oiseau 411833-2 OH), paired with the "Military" symphony (Symphony No. 100 in G Major).

Haydn's other well-known orchestral work is the Concerto in E-flat for Trumpet and Orchestra. Jazz trumpeter Wynton Marsalis released a brilliant interpretation of this work with the National Philharmonic Orchestra of London on Columbia Masterworks MK-37846. It garnered him a well-deserved classical-music Grammy Award (he was the first artist to win Grammys in both jazz and classical categories in the same year).

Chamber Works

The "Sun" quartets can be heard in their entirety on a two-CD set performed by the Tátrai Quartet (Hungaroton HCD 11332/ 33).

The most famous of Haydn's string quartets, including the "Emperor" and "Sunrise," are cataloged as Opus 76, a set of six works.

These are the first great modern quartets, in which the second violin, viola, and cello are raised out of a supporting role and given independent voices. There are many fine recordings of these works available, including the Amadeus Quartet (Deutsche Grammophon 415667-2 GCM2), the Tátrai Quartet (Hungaroton HCD 12812/13), both two-CD sets, and the Takacs Quartet (London 421360-2 LH and 425467-2 LH).

WOLFGANG AMADEUS MOZART

b. 1756, Salzburg, Austria
d. 1791, Vienna, Austria

Mozart's life and music have been so clouded with myth that it is difficult to separate fact from fiction. It is no exaggeration to say that he was a prodigious musical talent, one unequaled in the annals of music history. It is also no exaggeration to say that his life was filled with tragedy. But despite the tragic circumstances, he was able to produce a body of work that includes some of the greatest instrumental and vocal music ever conceived.

Leopold Mozart, Wolfgang's father, was a court musician for the Archbishop of Salzburg, a powerful political and religious figure in his native Austria. The elder Mozart was one of the first great German violinists, and he wrote the first violin instruction book ever published (coincidentally published the year of Wolfgang's birth). A composer and musician of no small talents, Leopold soon recognized in his son an extraordinary musical prodigy.

Wolfgang took an interest in his older sister's harpsichord lessons and, at the age of three, picked out melodies on the instrument. When Leopold began to instruct him on the instrument, he discovered that the boy had an incredible ear. He could reproduce melodies on a single hearing and play works by sight that would take others weeks, if not months, of practice. He could improvise on a single melody without repeating himself seemingly indefinitely.

By age five, Mozart was already attempting to compose music and, within a few years, he had written his first sonata and symphony. Mozart's compositions were every bit as amazing as his performance skills, showing remarkable maturity and a grasp of musical concepts that belied his years. Leopold was amazed by this great talent unfolding in his own household. He also must have recognized that the youngster was his ticket to great fame and fortune.

Leopold took the six-year-old Mozart on a performing trip to the courts of Vienna and Munich. This was the first of many performances for the young Mozart that would take him in the coming years to Versailles and London. The greatest nobility in Europe fawned and marveled over the child wonder. Public performances were also arranged, with something of a sideshow atmosphere creeping into the handbills distributed by the elder Mozart: "[Wolfgang] will play a concerto for the violin, and will accompany symphonies on the harpsichord, the manual or keyboard being covered with a cloth, with as much facility as if he could see the keys; he will instantly name all the notes played at a distance, whether singly or in chords on the harpsichord or any other instrument, bell, glass, or clock. He will finally improvise as long as may be desired, and in any key, on the harpsichord and organ."

Mozart's European travels ended in London in 1765, where he met the renowned composer Johann Christian Bach, the son of J. S. Bach who, at the time, was hailed as the greatest composer in all of Europe. Bach recognized the young musician's genius, while Mozart absorbed the Italianate musical style of the elder composer. It seemed there was no one, no matter how great, who did not immediately hail the youth's talents.

It must have been with some disappointment that the young man returned to his native Salzburg at age ten. Salzburg was hardly the center of great musical experimentation that London, Paris, or Vienna were. Moreover, the Mozart family was totally beholden to the powerful Archbishop, who employed Leopold. Without his permission, they could not continue their travels, and it was not clear that the Archbishop would continue to allow Leopold to travel with his son. He was skeptical of the many claims made for the child and demanded a new test. Wolfgang would be isolated in a room in his palace, given a text, and, within a short space of time, asked to compose an oratorio based on it. Apparently, Mozart's work did the trick, because the Archbishop had it published and performed at his own expense and granted permission for the family to travel again a year later.

Their trip to Vienna in 1767 forecast the problems Mozart would have as a young man. Once hailed as an adorable prodigy, the now eleven-year-old performer was no longer as attractive to the noblewomen. Furthermore, Vienna was in mourning because smallpox had taken the life of the young Archduchess, whose marriage festivities had already been planned. This tragedy left the nobility with little appetite for musical performances. Mozart did compose two operas, one of which, the short and charming *Bastien und Bastienne,* was given a private performance, winning the distinction of being Mozart's first opera that was performed.

Mozart spent a year in retirement in Salzburg, followed by a musical tour of Italy. He had to fight Italian prejudices against German musicians, who were felt to be at best copycats of the superior Italian artists. Despite these preconceptions, the Italians warmly embraced him. He was the youngest musician elected into the philharmonic academy of Bologna (at age fourteen) and was knighted by the Pope. The city of Milan invited him to compose an opera, *Mitridate, Rè di Ponto,* which premiered in December 1770. Despite the general feeling that no German could master the complex Italian operatic form, the work was hailed as a true work of genius and had an exceptional run of twenty performances.

The return to Salzburg was another letdown. A new Archbishop had been installed, one who treated Mozart father and son as merely hired hands. The stultifying atmosphere of the Salzburg court was obviously holding back the young composer's artistic growth; he knew he needed to seek employment in some more suitable city. At age twenty-one, he was given permission to travel again, but his father's request to accompany him was denied. Mozart's mother accompanied the young boy, whose ultimate destination would be Paris. Along the way he stopped in Mannheim, where he heard the remarkable orchestra led by Stamitz (see chapter 3) and also met Aloysia Weber, with whom he fell in love.

When they arrived in Paris, the Mozarts were shocked to be greeted by near-universal indifference. Now that Wolfgang was an adult, his amazing skills no longer amused. The only employment he was offered was as a lowly organist at Versailles, obviously a position beneath his dignity. To make matters worse, Mozart's mother became ill and died, leaving the young man alone for the first time in his life. He quickly retreated to Mannheim to reclaim Aloysia, but her ardor had cooled by the time he returned. He had no choice but to go back to Salzburg, his father, and the Archbishop.

Mozart's relations with the Archbishop continued to sour. He could not adapt himself to being anyone's servant, particularly to a man who had so little appreciation for his natural gifts. The final break came in 1781, when Mozart refused to deliver a letter for the Archbishop, a menial task that was beneath his dignity as a musician. At age twenty-four, he was finally his own man, breaking his ties with his hometown and his domineering father and employer.

Mozart settled in Vienna and had every expectation of a court appointment. His opera, *The Abduction from the Seraglio*, premiered in the summer of 1782 and was an immediate success. Only the antagonism of court composer Antonio Salieri marred its initial performances. Salieri sought to have the opera canceled, and his musicians attended its performances to boo and catcall. Still, the court in general was pleased with the work, and, with the hopes of soon having a lucrative post, Mozart wed Constanze Weber, the sister of his former beloved. It was also at this time that Mozart befriended Haydn and began composing the mature instrumental works that showed the deep influence of the elder composer's command of the classical vocabulary.

The last decade of Mozart's life was one of contradictions. On the one hand, he wrote some of the most beautiful and acclaimed music ever heard. His operas—*The Marriage of Figaro* and *Don Giovanni*—met with enormous success. A German composer had written the greatest Italian operas, and their performances were hailed as works of genius, despite the efforts of Salieri to sabotage them. But Mozart could not gain any permanent employment and was reduced to borrowing money from his friends to support himself and his ailing wife. A lesser man would have abandoned his musical career, but Mozart kept on composing despite his misfortunes and in spite of the fact that there was little, if any, opportunity for his works to be performed publicly.

In the last year of his life, Mozart finally had a court appointment, but the Viennese emperor perversely reduced the salary to keep the musician in relative poverty. Meanwhile, he worked feverishly on his opera *The Magic Flute*, which was commissioned by a local producer who wanted to stage a work in the German language for a popular audience. This work was the first great opera to appeal to a mass audience, and it is one of Mozart's best-loved works today.

The story of Mozart's death is the last great act of his life. The story goes that a mysterious, shrouded stranger showed up at Mozart's door early in 1792 with a commission for him to write a requiem. He was actually the servant of a Viennese count who often commissioned composers to write works that he would pass off later as his own. The secrecy and ominous aspect of the stranger deeply affected Mozart, and as he labored over the work he increasingly became convinced that he was writing his own funeral mass. The shrouded figure hounded him in his dreams, demanding that he complete the work before it was too late. Mozart, sadly, became too ill to complete it, although he did give one of his students instructions on how to bring it to an end.

Mozart's funeral was a sad footnote to his earlier fame. He was given a pauper's burial in an unmarked grave. His widow was too grief-stricken to attend. His archrival Salieri ironically led the funeral band. Because a cold rain was falling, the few mourners who attended the church service elected not to follow the casket to the graveyard. Years later, no one could identify where exactly the greatest composer of the time had been buried.

Of Mozart, Madonna, and Money

Genius is unrewarded, says the old saw, and for years we believed that Mozart scraped out his life barely eking out a living. Now, new evidence has been offfered by New York University husband-and-wife economists William and Hilda Baumol, evidence that strongly suggests that Mozart was actually well-paid for his endeavors.

During the last decade of his life, Mozart lived and worked in Vienna, making an annual salary that averaged about 2,000 florins. Using a complex formula, the Baumols figure that a florin is roughly equivalent to $10 today, making this figure about $20,000 a year. When you figure in income from performing, teaching, and publishing, the Baumols guesstimate that Mozart averaged about $35,000 a year.

And don't forget, there's been considerable inflation since the days of old Vienna. A florin just doesn't buy what it used to! The Baumols figure that today's dollar is worth at least 85 percent less in actual buying power than the comparable amount would have been 200 years ago. This means that Mozart's pocket change would have bought approximately six and two-thirds more goods than current dollars.

How is it that Mozart (and his contemporary musicians) were able to make so much more than the average laboring man? Three trends helped increase the demand for musical compositions. Austria-Germany at this time was a complex spiderweb of little duchies, each with its own ruler. Some 1,800 courts needed court musicians, and each demanded unique music. Mozart, of course, was unlucky in his pursuit of a court appointment until late in his life. The second trend was the growth of the middle class, fueled by banking and trade. These tradesmen would finance musical compositions, attend concerts, and become music students themselves. Finally, new technologies, such as the invention of the pianoforte, made it possible for music to be performed in larger concert halls. This meant that bigger audiences could gather to hear the music, and their contributions through ticket prices could be used to pay for musical compositions and performances.

How does Mozart's income stack up with that of a contemporary musical star such as Madonna? While Mozart made $35,000 in a good year, Madonna made $23,000,000 in fiscal year 1990. New technologies are to be thanked for the increase in income. While Mozart was limited to performing for the Viennese audience, Madonna's image is beamed worldwide through MTV and films. In fact, she made almost as much through film and video production in 1990 as she did through record sales and music-publishing royalties ($10,000,000 for video/film, $13,000,000 for records/music). If Mozart had had access to MTV, CDs, films, and licensing possibilities, he undoubtedly would have been far wealthier. Then again, Mozart's $35,000 was tax-free; Madonna has to cough up about 30 percent of her income for taxes (less any deductions), plus pay agent's fees, publicists, bodyguards, and staff members.

If Mozart was so wealthy, you might wonder why he was buried in a pauper's grave. The Baumols have an answer for this troubling question, perhaps the most bizarre of all their findings. Apparently, Emperor Joseph II of Austria decided that, in a rational world, there was no need to honor the dead with individual graves and false lamenting. Instead, he advocated mass graves. The aristocracy was anxious to please him, and many upper-crust lords and ladies were buried anonymously for a while in common, unmarked holes. After a while, the bodies were surreptitiously reburied in fancier digs. Perhaps this is why Mozart's body was buried anonymously, never to be identified again.

Thought question: If Mozart had been able to earn royalties through his compositions, as modern composers do, how much would his estate have been worth at the time of his death? How much income would his music still produce every year?

Heavy-duty thought question: If Mozart had placed 3,000 florins in a Certificate of Deposit earning 7.5 percent income on average for 200 years at the time of his death, how much would that account be worth today? Hint: It would be more than enough to buy the wedding gown used on the cover of Madonna's *Like A Virgin* LP at auction (the gown recently sold for $11,000).

Recommended Listening

Despite poverty, ill health, and the ups and downs of his career, Mozart was a remarkably prolific composer, showing talent in a variety of styles. He composed about forty symphonies; twenty piano concerti; seventeen solo piano sonatas; various concerti for other instruments, including violin, clarinet, flute, and bassoon; string quartets; and miscellaneous orchestral works such as divertissements, serenades, and nocturnes. His great operatic works fall outside the scope of this book.

Overviews

Many recordings were issued in 1991 to celebrate the 200th anniversary of Mozart's death. For those who want a general one-stop overview of Mozart's musical life, there are several good collections. *Amadeus Mozart* presents the works by Mozart featured in the popular film *Amadeus* (Columbia Masterworks MDK 46578). For the budget-minded, there is *The Magic of Mozart* (Vox/Turnabout PVT 7110), featuring mostly Eastern European recordings. Columbia Masterworks has issued two CDs of *Mozart's Greatest Hits* (MLK 39436; 45813), featuring major American and European artists who have recorded for Masterworks over the last thirty years. For the completist, there is the budget-priced five-CD set on Sony Classical SBK 45977 called *The Compact Mozart*; this gives a representative sampling of Mozart's works in their entirety. For those who prefer their Mozart in bite-sized portions, there's *100 Mozart Melodies* (Sony Classical SBK 46240), another specially priced five-disc set, featuring snippets of the best-loved tunes that set Wolfgang a-hummin'. Finally, for those who can't stop boppin', there's the Swingle Singers a cappella renditions of Mozart's popular melodies on *A Cappella Amadeus* (Virgin Classics 7 91208-2).

Orchestral Music

Mozart wrote his first "symphony" at the age of seven, although this early work was not in the modern symphonic form. His last symphony was written three years before his death. His best-known symphonic works were written in the period from 1782 to 1788, six works that are the culmination of his skills as a symphonic composer and are often performed today.

One of Mozart's most popular symphonies is the Symphony No. 35 in D Major, "Haffner," K. 385,* written to order for the burgomaster (or mayor) of Salzburg, Sigmund Haffner. The piece has considerable grace and charm, particularly in the two middle sections, where strings and woodwinds trade pastoral melodies. The opening section is unique in the orchestral repertoire in that it has only one theme. At the point that a second theme would normally appear, the first theme is repeated instead, but transposed to a different key. A historic recording of this work from the late '30s, conducted by Sir Thomas Beecham leading the London Philharmonic Orchestra, is available on a three-CD set (Angel CDHC 63698) along with several other Mozart symphonies. Deutsche Grammophon has issued two recordings of the "Haffner" by Leonard Bernstein leading the Vienna Philharmonic Orchestra (429521-2 GMF and 431039-2 GBE). Christopher Hogwood and

---

*The "K" numbers used to catalog Mozart's works refer to the work of Ludwig von Köchel (1800–1877), the first scholar to organize and number Mozart's works in chronological order.

the Academy of Ancient Music perform the work on period instruments on London 417760-2 LM.

Another well-loved Mozart symphony is the so-called "Prague," Symphony No. 38 in D Major, K. 504, composed in 1786. Its name comes from the city where it was premiered and received as a masterwork. In its many charming melodies and masterful use of orchestral colors it shows the influence of Mozart's dramatic compositions *The Marriage of Figaro* and *Don Giovanni*, which were composed at the same time. Unlike other symphonies, the work lacks a third movement or minuet, which is quite remarkable since Mozart was a master of the minuet form. It can be heard on the Sir Thomas Beecham set and the second Bernstein CD listed in the previous paragraph. Herbert von Karajan and the Berlin Philharmonic perform it on a three-CD set, along with a selection of Mozart's other well-loved orchestral works (including the "Haffner"), on Deutsche Grammophon 429668-2 GSE3.

For some reason, Mozart feverishly produced three symphonies in just six weeks in 1788. It is not known whether he had a specific commission with an incredibly short deadline or whether he simply felt compelled to produce these last great compositions. The best-known is the final work, known as "Jupiter," Symphony No. 41 in C Major, K. 551. It gained this name because of its majestic nature, marked by the dramatic chords of its opening movement, and the beautifully conceived finale, with its powerful counterpoint that illustrates Mozart's mastery of the orchestra. The work has often been recorded. George Szell and the Cleveland Orchestra perform it, along with "Haffner," on Sony Classical SBK 46333, and Claudio Abbado conducts the London Symphony in a modern version of this work on Deutsche Grammophon 429801-2. It is also featured on Angel CDHC 63698, the historic three-CD set by Sir Thomas Beecham and the London Philharmonic.

Besides symphonies, Mozart composed several less formal orchestral works. These works had no particular overriding form and went by various names, such as nocturnes and serenades. They were often written for a specific event, to provide background music for the celebrations of the nobility and middle class.

The most famous of these works is "Eine kleine Nachtmusik" (Serenade in G Major, K. 525), a serenade in four movements. There are more than fifty recordings of this well-loved work, including CDs by the Amadeus Quartet (Deutsche Grammophon 400065-2), Sir Neville Marriner and the Academy of Saint Martin-in-the-Fields (London 417741-2), and James Galway with the Chamber Orchestra of Europe on a two-CD set with various other works (RCA 7861-2-RC).

Quartets and Other Instrumental Works

Mozart composed some twenty-five string quartets, but the greatest were six written between 1782 and 1785, influenced by and dedicated to Haydn. They outstrip all of Mozart's earlier works in this form and represent the greatest achievement up to that time in compositional form, use of the four unique instrumental voices, and expression of lyricism and deep emotion. They can be heard on a budget-priced three-CD set performed by the Juilliard Quartet (Odyssey MB3K 45826). They are also available individually or paired with one or two of Mozart's other works on various recordings.

It's not surprising that Mozart wrote many pieces featuring the newly introduced pianoforte, for it was an instrument that he had mastered. When he settled in Vienna, he was invited to a challenge concert with the great pianist Muzio Clementi, universally recognized as the best living pianist in Europe. Mozart did not win, but the judges ruled the match a tie, an amazing achievement for the younger musician.

Among Mozart's piano works are seventeen solo piano sonatas, about twenty piano concerti, and over forty sonatas for violin and piano. The concerti are unique in that the piano is better integrated into the orchestra than in earlier works. Mozart treated the piano as an equal to the other orchestral voices, greatly influencing Beethoven's piano works. In his sonatas for violin and piano, particularly the twenty or so written earlier in his career, the piano takes the dominant role, again reflecting Mozart's interest in the instrument.

The complete Mozart piano sonatas can be heard performed by

Daniel Barenboim on a six-CD set (Angel CDCF-47335). Malcolm Bilson, a noted player of a reproduction of an early piano similar in dynamics and range to the instruments of Mozart's time, has recorded the sonatas on two separately sold two-CD sets (Hungaraton HCD-31009/10 and 31011/12). Glenn Gould's dramatic reading of these works is available on two budget-priced two-CD sets (Odyssey MB2K 45612 and 45613). There are also single CDs featuring various combinations of the individual sonatas by almost every major pianist.

The complete piano concerti fill nine or more CDs, depending on how they are packaged! An interesting recording featuring period instruments, with several pianists including the talented Malcolm Bilson, is available on a nine-CD set on Deutsche Grammophon 431211-2 AX9. For the more frugally minded, the concerti are available individually or paired with other Mozart works on recordings by pianists such as Murray Perahia, Rudolf Serkin, Peter Serkin, Vladimir Ashkenazy, Alfred Brendel, and most other major pianists.

How Do You Stack Up with Mozart?

As a public service, and to make you feel worse than you already do, we offer this schematic chart of the life and achievements of W. A. Mozart compared with the fictional Ordinary Joe of today.

Age	Mozart	Ordinary Joe
3	Shows interest in the harpsichord	Begins toilet training
4	Begins music lessons	Begins nursery school
5	Writes harpsichord minuet	Enrolls in kindergarten
6	Makes first tour to Munich and Vienna	Makes first trip to Disneyland
7	Performs for French king at Versailles; writes first sonata	Enters second grade; learns to tie his own shoes
8	Performs in London and Paris; writes first symphony	Enters third grade; stars as a tree in class play
10	Composes first oratorio	Sings "America" in school assembly

11	Gets smallpox; writes first opera	Gets Lyme disease
14	Tours Italy; knighted by Pope; composes second opera	Enters high school; gets first adult-sized bike
17	Continues to tour Europe; composes concerti and string quartets	Enters college; wins beer-drinking contest at local bar
21	Begins another European tour	Graduates from college; hired to manage local Woolworth's
25	Meets Haydn and greatly influences his music; composes another opera	Loses first job after sleeping with the cashier
26	Marries Constanze Weber; writes "Haffner" symphony, another opera, and three piano concerti	Marries Josephine Ordinaire; buys lawn mower
29	Composes *The Marriage of Figaro*	Starts going bald
30	Writes a piano sonata, two string quartets, and a piano concerto	Helps brother-in-law move his piano
31	Composes *Don Giovanni*	Divorces wife; buys leisure suit
32	Composes three famous symphonies (including "Jupiter")	Gets job selling used cars
35	Composes *The Magic Flute;* dies	Arrested for consumer fraud; trial pending

SEVEN
FROM CLASSICAL
TO ROMANTIC

The next revolution in music came in the period from 1780 to 1850, when the new "Romantic" music came into being. Romantic music was not born overnight, but once it took hold, it became a force in European art that has lasted up to our time.

The Romantic movement was a reaction to the earlier Classical style. As is so often the case in history, revolutions are born out of the discontent of a new generation with the beliefs of their elders. (The outrageousness of punk rock was inspired by punkers' beliefs that older rock acts had bought into the star system and become musically stale.) A brief review of the central Classical beliefs will help us to understand what the Romantics were rebelling against.

The Classical artist valued order, symmetry, and formal beauty as the goals of creativity. A square is a beautiful form, it is perfectly symmetrical and expresses certain abstract mathematical laws. For the Classical composer, to express perfectly the symphonic form, for example, was the ultimate achievement. Bach's "Art of the Fugue" is an exploration of the fugal form through all of its many intricacies, and as such it's an exploration and triumphant expression of the Classical aesthetic.

As an aside, I might note that interpretation can also play a role in how we view a work of art. Glenn Gould made a famous recording of "Art of the Fugue" in 1962 that revived interest in this work. He approached it as a Romantic, giving a highly emotive performance, changing what were previously viewed as dull academic exercises into a moving work of art, from the Romantic perspective. To hear this recording, buy Columbia Masterworks M2K-42270 (a two-CD set that also includes other Bach works).

The Classic/Romantic Test

Are you the kind of person who keeps your socks in the socks drawer? Or are you a free spirit who keeps your undies in the glove box of your VW Bug? This may make a difference in the kind of music that you enjoy. So, as a public service, we present the Classic/Romantic Test, a quick and dirty way to tell what kind of composer you'd enjoy most (with apologies to F. Parvin Sharpless who devised a more elaborate test for his book *Romanticism: A Literary Perspective*, Rochelle Park, NJ: Hayden, 1979).

1. My front lawn at home is
   - (a) a neatly kept, mowed expanse of green grass
   - (b) riddled with wildflowers and weeds
   - (c) overgrown and populated with wild animals and rusty tin cans
   - (d) divided into four squares: one with flowers, one with a small waterfall, one with herbs, and one with a rock garden

2. I like movies where
   - (a) the good guy wins and the bad guy loses
   - (b) a big monster destroys helpless people
   - (c) uplifting thoughts are expressed
   - (d) mutant teenagers take over their high school and dance naked in the cafeteria

3. My high-school science teacher was great because
   - (a) every day we'd do something new
   - (b) she always gave us an outline for each class
   - (c) she was open to an individual student's suggestions
   - (d) she set high standards for us to meet

4. When I take the laundry out of the dryer, I immediately
   - (a) throw it in a big ball in my bottom dresser drawer
   - (b) roll all of the socks neatly together
   - (c) sew missing buttons on all the shirts and hang them up neatly
   - (d) go out for a pizza

5. To me, sex is
   (a) a biological function necessary to continue the human race
   (b) the highest expression of the human spirit
   (c) as much fun as roller skating, and less dangerous
   (d) overrated

6. When a composer writes a piece of music, he or she is primarily interested in
   (a) expressing deep emotions
   (b) working out a satisfying musical form
   (c) gaining worldwide fame and fortune
   (d) building on the traditions of earlier composers

7. My favorite writer is
   (a) Norman Mailer
   (b) Alexander Pope
   (c) Sylvia Plath
   (d) John McPhee

8. The best place to meet people is
   (a) on a subway car
   (b) at a class reunion
   (c) at a bar
   (d) at work

9. I think all poetry should
   (a) rhyme and be written in regular lines
   (b) tell us something about the poet's life
   (c) teach us how to live
   (d) be free-form, without any regular rhythm

10. The first thing I think when I wake up each morning is
   (a) everything is right with the world
   (b) oh shit, another morning
   (c) today is the first day of the rest of my life
   (d) today is the last day of my old life and the first day of my new life

Scoring

Total your score based on the following information:

1. Classicists like order, so take 50 points if you checked d, 25 points if you chose a. Romantics are sloppy, so subtract 50 points if you chose c, and 25 points if you chose b.

2. Classicists like order (a, plus 50) or art with a purpose (c, plus 25). Romantics like the free expression of passion (d, minus 50) or the struggle of the individual versus society (b, minus 25).
3. Romantics like freedom and the unexpected (a, minus 50), where each individual can contribute (c, minus 25). Classicists like order (b, plus 50), where each person is expected to conform to an external standard (d, plus 25).
4. The Classicist likes to organize and improve (b, plus 50; c, plus 25); the Romantic doesn't seek to organize (a, minus 50; d, minus 25).
5. Sex for the Classicist is a necessary evil (a, plus 50; d, plus 25). For the Romantic, sex brings man closer to God (b, minus 50) and it's fun to boot (c, minus 25).
6. The Romantic composer is aiming for personal expression (a, minus 50) or to gain recognition (c, minus 25); the Classicist seeks to continue traditional forms (b, plus 50; d, plus 25).
7. Mailer is the ultimate Romantic hothead (a, minus 50); Plath made poetry out of her own suffering (c, minus 25). Pope is the ultimate Classicist, writing perfectly rhymed couplets (b, plus 50); McPhee also is a Classicist, documenting the external world and giving it order (d, plus 25).
8. Classicists believe in social order; they socialize only within their own class or group (b, plus 50; d, plus 25). Romantics look for friends among the riffraff (a, minus 50; c, minus 25); all men are noble!
9. Classicists go for order in poetry (a, plus 50) or for poetry with a message (c, plus 25). Romantics go for confessional poetry (b, minus 50) and freedom (d, minus 25).
10. Classicists see the world as static and good (a, plus 50; c, plus 25). Romantics see the world as dynamic and changing (d, minus 75). Pessimists just can't get out of bed (b)!

To Score:

Plus 500 would be a perfect Classicist; minus 500 would be an incurable Romantic. Locate yourself on the following scale:

500	So perfect as to be inhuman
400	Kind of a drip, but well organized
300	Intellectual and astute
200	A smarty-pants
100	Having a few good qualities
zero	Unable to make up your mind
-100	Dashing, occasionally
-200	A free spirit, constrained by social pressures

-300 A wild Irish rose
-400 Painfully sensitive and acutely aware of the woes of the world
-500 Lord Byron, P. B. Shelley, and John Keats rolled into one!

By using this scale, you can determine how you rate as a Romantic or Classicist and apply it to your listening habits. For example, if your score is 378, you should stick to Bach; if it's -434, you'd better dust off the Schubert.

Classical artists saw themselves as servants of their society. Thus, musicians such as Haydn were happy to be no more than indentured servants to their patrons. After all, the social order dictated that musicians serve their employers, and not vice versa. The government itself was subservient to the church, which expressed the superhuman or divine order. So a hierarchy of God-church-government-individual was established, itself a perfect order that was to be obeyed by each person as he or she fit into the divine plan.

The Romantics burst through these beliefs. They saw the highest expression of the individual to be his or her own individuality. God was not over individuals, He was within them. Thus, humans expressed their godliness by being themselves. Governments were not validated by some divine plan, but rather by how they served the people. Democracy, or the voice of the people, was the ultimate form of self-government. Through voting, the people dictated the laws and then chose to follow them.

Romantic music follows these dictates. Music is not an expression of an abstract form or ideal; rather, it is an exploration of our inner emotions. Thus, feelings should dictate form, not vice versa. The musician, as a person in touch with our deepest feelings, is a special person, and does not need to be subservient to anyone. The patron should serve the musician, not vice versa.

From Classical to Romantic

For the sake of clarity, we've divided the history of music into periods: Early/Medieval; Baroque; Classical; Romantic; and Modern. But, like all historical divisions, these are somewhat arbitrary, and there comes a point where music historians disagree over when one period ends and another begins. After all, these designations were made after the fact, not while the actual history was being made. In trying to make order out of historical chaos, it is tempting to forget the immortal words "Life is just one damn thing after another"; or, in the words of Henry Ford, "History is bunk"!

The Romantic period did not begin all at once; it was the culmination of trends in society and the arts over more than a century. The first shots fired against organized religion were made by Martin Luther in 1517. In government, kings began to wobble and fall from the 1600s through the 1800s. So, it is not surprising to find figures in this era that straddle the gap between the Romantic and Classical.

Beethoven and Schubert are two figures who fall into this category. For some historians, Beethoven represents the culmination of the Classical era. His symphonies were the most highly developed compositions of their time and were a model of the symphonic form for the next generation of composers. On the other hand, Beethoven can also be viewed as a fiery Romantic: in temperament, he was highly emotional; he did not suffer fools gladly or kowtow to his patrons; and his great works expressed a depth of emotion that was rarely heard before in classical music. His sentiments were clearly on the side of the common man and individual liberty, and away from the ancient hierarchy of church and state that had ruled Europe for hundreds of years.

Schubert is also a transitional figure. His life story reads like a Romantic stereotype: friendly with bohemian artists, he led a dissolute life of loafs, ladies, and lieder, not to mention artistic discussions and debates, ending tragically in his death from syphilis. Schubert produced music at a feverish pace, almost as if he had a premonition that he did not have long to make his mark. And the music he produced lies somewhere in the no-man's-land between the Classical and Romantic: formally beautiful, but also emotionally deep. Not yet breaking through all of the chains that bound the Classical composers, Schubert points the way, in his life and music, for the next generation of Romantic composers.

LUDWIG VAN BEETHOVEN

b. 1770, Bonn, Germany
d. 1827, Vienna, Austria

Beethoven was born in the shadow of Mozart, in more ways than one. His alcoholic father, a small-time musician, recognized his son's musical capabilities and hoped to market him to the new popular audience, just as Leopold Mozart had made a success with his son. To this end, he forced the young Beethoven to practice the piano night and day, ironically stunting his natural talents. The more the boy was worked, the more unevenly he played, perhaps because he was so overly tired and frightened of his domineering father. His concert debut at the age of eight (his father advertised his age as six, in an attempt, no doubt, to make his performance that much more "amazing") was a dud.

The first sympathetic ear for the young musician was the local court organist Christian Gottlob Neefe. Although Beethoven's development was erratic, Neefe believed in the boy, making him his assistant and raising the money for Beethoven to make his first trip to Vienna to meet the legendary Mozart. The nervous young musician was introduced to Mozart, who at first was unimpressed with his untidy appearance and halting performance. Mozart decided to give the youngster a final chance to show his skills. He played a theme for Beethoven that he had never heard before, and challenged him to improvise on it. When the young musician was finished, a sobered Mozart predicted that he would "make a big noise" in the musical world.

Beethoven returned home to a deteriorating family situation. His mother, who had been a sympathetic buffer between him and his demanding father, was dying. His father was lapsing further into alcoholism, and it was up to Beethoven as the eldest son to support the family. He quickly obtained a position as a violist in the local theater orchestra. Other local musicians contributed extra cash to the family.

Beethoven was fortunate to have a friend in a local aristocrat,

Count Waldstein. Believing in the young man's genius, he arranged for him to study with one of the greatest musicians of the day, Franz Joseph Haydn. Haydn had passed through Bonn in 1790, heard Beethoven, and enthusiastically praised his capabilities. He invited him to come to Vienna as his student. Waldstein was instrumental in raising the necessary capital for a trip to Vienna, along with enough funds to provide for food and lodging. The death of Mozart in 1791 convinced Waldstein that Beethoven had a special mission in life: to complete the legacy of the other great German composer. He told Beethoven when he left for Vienna: "Mozart's guardian angel still mourns and weeps over the death of his charge. . . . You shall receive Mozart's spirit from the hands of Haydn."

When Beethoven arrived in Vienna, he was still a small-town boy who dressed poorly and did not have many social skills. On the other hand, Beethoven's offhand style was an expression of his deeper feelings that he was a special person, set apart from the common man, who did not have the time or inclination to participate in the social niceties. Beethoven's ambivalence toward society expressed itself in his hot temper and pride; he did not easily take the criticism of others.

Beethoven was an erratic musician, but he appears to have been a great improviser on the piano. He was able to improvise on a theme for hours, always inventing something new and showing amazing technique on the relatively new instrument. Often bored and surly when presented with a finished composition to "perform," Beethoven seems to have been happiest when given the opportunity to let his genius freely express itself, without limitations.

Beethoven's relations with his mentor and teacher Haydn expressed all of these ambiguities. Although Haydn greatly admired his talents, he was unable to control the younger musician. Coming from an earlier generation that expected reverence and deference to elders, Haydn was shocked and confused by Beethoven's behavior. Eventually he abandoned his student, hoping that other hands could work more successfully with him. But Beethoven proved too difficult for all of his teachers, and he had to strike out on his own.

Thanks to Count Waldstein, he had letters of introduction to many of the Viennese aristocrats. Beethoven was quickly able to obtain employment as a teacher and composer for special occasions, such as weddings, private parties, or funerals. The year 1800 was an important, but unfortunate, one for him. His first symphony was premiered in Vienna. Sadly, Beethoven was unable to afford to hire musicians of a sufficient caliber to perform his works, and the critics were unable to distinguish between the quality of the work and the shortcomings of its performance.

A second catastrophe came at the end of 1800, when Beethoven discovered he was going deaf. His livelihood as a musician was threatened; he feared if his patrons discovered his growing disability, they would cease to give him commissions. Obviously, his days as a performer were numbered. Yet, the hardheaded composer was determined to continue, and his disability became, in a strange way, an asset. The less Beethoven could hear, the harder he worked at perfecting his skills as a composer. He had to develop unusual capabilities for constructing his works on paper, because he could not control their performance.

In the period from 1801 to 1812, the composer produced some of his most famous works, including the "Moonlight" sonata, the "Eroica" (third symphony), and the famous fifth symphony. Despite his productivity, Beethoven continued to be moody, although his aristocratic friends did not waver in their support of him. Then, for five years Beethoven fell into a slump, producing little. This fallow period led to his final burst of creativity, from 1817 to his death in 1827.

The greatest work of this last period was the ninth symphony, capped with the uplifting "Ode to Joy." The story of this work's premiere is another testimony to Beethoven's determination and egotism. He insisted on conducting, even though he could no longer hear. When the piece was completed, the composer went on conducting, oblivious to the fact that the orchestra had ceased playing. This pathetic sight so moved the audience that they leapt to their feet, recognizing the tremendous effort that he had made.

Unlike Bach and Mozart, who died in poverty and unappreciated, Beethoven's death in 1827 was greeted by mass mourning.

The German people realized they had lost a unique and important voice. The musical world was now the property of the general public, and the public participated in this first great loss of a new era of musical creation.

Recommended Listening

Overviews

There are several recordings that give good overviews of Beethoven's best-loved works. *Greatest Hits, Volumes One* and *Two* (Columbia Masterworks MLK-39434; MLK-45812) draw on the extensive Columbia Masterworks library of recordings of well-known orchestras and soloists in a selection of excerpts and complete works. Pro Arte has issued a midpriced collection, called *Beethoven's Greatest Hits*, CDM-820, consisting of excerpts from his better-known works. For those who like their Beethoven served up with hot sauce, there's Don Dorsey's *Beethoven or Bust* featuring favorite works played on synthesizer (Telarc CD80153).

Orchestral Works

Beethoven is most famous for his nine symphonies, particularly the fifth and his final work. Although his first two symphonies showed the clear influence of 18th-century composers such as Mozart and Haydn, the remainder (with the exception of the eighth symphony) are clearly products of a new and fundamentally different imagination. Beethoven was the first great symphonic artist, using the orchestra like a vast palette to paint his pictures of joy, heroism, grandeur, and grief. He used a wider variety of instruments than his predecessors, introducing the modern orchestra in all of its voices. He used the individual instrumental voices more creatively, calling for changes in volume, attack, and texture. His use of dissonant or unusual harmonies was far more daring than his contemporaries', and he used modulation, or changing from key to key, in a more free and radical manner than his predecessors. He also added new parts to the symphonic format, including the scherzo, a light-hearted movement, in place of the minuet, and even a funeral march in the famous third symphony. Beethoven viewed the symphony as a narrative art, and he was unafraid to exploit the many techniques at his disposal.

There are many fine complete sets of Beethoven's symphonies. Herbert von Karajan recorded the complete symphonies twice as the leader of the Berlin Philharmonic, in the early '60s and again in the mid-'70s (Deutsche Grammophon 429036-2 GX5; 429089-2 GSE6); the earlier recordings are re-issued on five CDs, the later on six. An even earlier von Karajan reading with the Philharmonia Orchestra from the early '50s is available on five CDs on Angel CDME-63310. Arturo Toscanini's historic recording with the NBC Symphony is re-issued on five CDs on RCA Gold Seal 60324-2-RG. Leonard Bernstein's version, conducting the Vienna Philharmonic Orchestra, is available on six CDs (Deutsche Grammophon 427306-2 GH6).

The third symphony, popularly known as the "Eroica," was Beethoven's celebration of the new waves of freedom sweeping across Europe. Originally dedicated to Napoleon, the composer changed the work's name when he realized that Napoleon intended to make himself emperor. Beethoven wished to celebrate man's heroism as he overthrew tyrants, not the establishment of new tyranny. The entire work expresses a deeply emotional and troubled feeling, from the powerful opening chords, the juxtaposition of dissonant harmonies and sweetly harmonized, quieter passages, the unusual introduction of a deeply felt funeral march as the work's second movement, through the finale featuring a fugue used to express the turmoil that was occurring on the European political stage. Some noteworthy recordings of the "Eroica" include Leonard Bernstein with the New York Philharmonic (Columbia Masterworks MK-42220), Neville Marriner and the Academy of Saint Martin-in-the-Fields (Philips 410044-2), George Szell and the Cleveland Orchestra (Sony Classical SBK 46328), and Herbert von Karajan and the Berlin Philharmonic Orchestra (Deutsche Grammophon 415506-2 GH or 419049-2 GGA).

Probably no four notes are more famous than the "da-da-da-daa" that open Beethoven's fifth symphony. The sound of these notes and their rhythmic pattern resonates throughout the symphony, now played by one instrument or section, then another, always gathering intensity and feeling. Beethoven even used the kettledrums to beat out the rhythm in the work's finale, a unique use of these instruments that were previously primarily used for special effects. He also makes melodic use of the double basses in the final movement as an important voice in the dramatic fugue. There are many fine recordings of the fifth symphony available, including Vladimir Ashkenazy conducting the Philharmonia Orchestra (London 40060-2 LH), Zubin Mehta leading the New York Philharmonic (Columbia Masterworks MT-35892), Christopher Hogwood and the Academy of Ancient Music (Oiseau 417615-2 OH), and André Previn and the Royal Philharmonic Orchestra (RCA Red Seal 7894-2-RC).

The ninth symphony is best known for its finale, the famous "Ode to Joy." Introducing a chorus into a symphonic work was a major innovation, and yet one that makes perfect sense in this great masterpiece. The entire final movement shows Beethoven's incredible craft and command of the orchestra. It opens with a recapitulation of all of the themes in the previous movements, as if the composer were searching for the appropriate introduction to the famous chorus. Then, the magnificent theme is heard in the basses and cellos, moving up the scale to the violas, and finally the violins. The orchestra breaks into the melody with a burst of power, heralding the first vocal soloist, who is joined by three other voices in a quartet, and finally the entire chorus enters to proclaim the joyous message of Friedrich von Schiller's poem, which served as the text of the choral section.

Again, there are a multitude of fine recordings of this work from which to choose. You might start with Leonard Bernstein's version recorded live in East Berlin in 1989 for its great emotional impact that came as much from the time and place of recording as from the musicianship involved (Deutsche Grammophon 429861-2 GH). Also noteworthy are Herbert von Karajan's 1984 recording (a two-CD set including the fifth symphony; Deutsche Grammophon 413933-4 GH2), and Zubin Mehta leading the New York Philharmonic with the New York Choral Artists, including soloists Marilyn Horne and Margaret Price (RCA Silver Seal 60477-2-RV).

Besides the symphonies, Beethoven composed overtures used as "curtain raisers" for various dramatic productions. He also wrote several concerti, most notably five concerti for piano and orchestra. The piano concerti show a definite development, with the first three still in the shadow of Mozart. The piano part is separated from the orchestra and is designed as a showpiece for the technical virtuosity of the pianist. The final two concerti, written in 1806 and 1809, respectively, are more like the mature Beethoven symphonies, as the piano and orchestra work together for a unified effect. There are none of the flashy pyrotechnics of the earlier works. The concerti are available on complete sets and individually. All of the complete collections are three-CD sets, including Claudio Arrau and the Dresden State Orchestra (Philips 422149-2 PH3); Vladimir Ashkenazy and the Cleveland Orchestra (London 421819-2 LH3); Alfred Brendel and the Chicago Symphony, a live recording (Philips 411189-2 PH3); and Murray Perahia with the Royal Concertgebouw Orchestra of Holland (Columbia Masterworks M3K-44575).

Piano and Chamber Works

Beethoven was a great pianist, one of the first composers to truly explore the instrument's capabilities. He composed thirty-two piano sonatas in all. We can trace his development from the early works (written in the 1790s) that show the influence of Haydn to the mature works that show a depth of feeling and a command of technique that puts Beethoven far ahead of earlier masters. Perhaps his best-known work is the so-called "Moonlight" sonata, in which Beethoven stretches the sonata form with a free-form structure and flowing, highly emotional melodies. The sonatas are available both on complete sets and on individual CDs. Complete sets worthy of note include Daniel Barenboim's recordings, split into two six-CD sets (Deutsche Grammophon 413759-2 GX6; 413766-2 GX6), Alfred Brendel's eleven-CD set (Philips 412575-2 PH11), and Arthur Schnabel's historic recordings from 1932 to 1935 rereleased on eight CDs (Angel CDHH-63765). Three of the best-loved sonatas, the "Moonlight," "Pathétique," and "Appassionata," are packaged together on recordings by Claudio Arrau (Philips 422970-2 PB), Van Cliburn (along with Sonata 26, known as "Les Adieux"; RCA Gold Seal 60356-2-RG), Vladimir Horowitz (Columbia Masterworks MK-34509), and Rudolf Serkin (Columbia Masterworks MYK-37219).

In addition to the solo piano sonatas, Beethoven wrote ten sonatas that he said were "for pianoforte with the accompaniment of the violin." Turning the traditional roles upside down, Beethoven treated the two instruments as equals rather than using the piano merely as a backup to the violinist. The best-known work of this group is popularly known as the "Kreutzer" sonata, after the French violinist Rodolphe Kreutzer (1766–1831), who won Beethoven's admiration when he was living in Vienna. It is not known whether Kreutzer ever performed the work that immortalized him. Good recordings of this work, along with the fifth sonata, known as "Spring," feature Itzhak Perlman and Vladimir Ashkenazy (London 410554-2 LH) and Pinchas Zukerman and Daniel Barenboim (Angel CDM 49817) on violin and piano, respectively.

Beethoven composed sixteen string quartets, which are divided by music scholars into three groups: the early quartets that recall the Classical models of Mozart and Haydn; the middle quartets, composed about 1806 and sharing with other works of this period a stormy emotionality; and the final group, written between 1825 and 1826, which have a serenity and deep composure that is unlike anything else in the Beethoven canon. The early works, known as Opus 18, can be heard on a pair of three-CD sets, one by the Juilliard Quartet (Columbia Masterworks M3K-37868) and the other by the Guarneri Quartet (RCA Gold Seal 60456-2-RG). Opus 59, consisting of three quartets, and Opus 74 and 95, are considered the middle-period works; they can be heard on a three-CD set by the Tokyo String Quartet (RCA Red Seal 60462-2-RC). The final works are available on recordings by the Melos Quartet (Deutsche Grammophon 415676-2 GH3) and the Juilliard Quartet (Columbia Masterworks M3K-37873), both three-CD collections.

FRANZ SCHUBERT

b. 1797, Vienna, Austria
d. 1828, Vienna, Austria

Franz Schubert was a Romantic character, flouting social norms to lead a bohemian existence. In his short life he was remarkably prolific, although most of his musical works were unknown during his lifetime. But, after his death, his works were discovered by important musicians such as Robert Schumann and Felix Mendelssohn and were influential on the growth of Romanticism.

Schubert was the son of a poor parish schoolmaster. Although his father enjoyed amateur music-making, he had no ambitions for himself or his children beyond the schoolyard. Young Franz showed remarkable talents on the piano and violin. His first teacher marveled at his ability, saying "He seems to know each lesson perfectly before I can begin explaining it to him." His teacher urged the elder Schubert to allow the boy to audition for the Imperial Chapel choir school, which would offer him an excellent education plus food and lodging. The famous composer Antonio Salieri was one of the teachers there. Schubert's father assented, and the boy auditioned at age eleven and was speedily admitted to the school.

School life was hard. Schubert was a withdrawn pupil, enjoying only music-making and singing. He did not socialize easily with the other boys, who looked down at him because of his humble background. Plus, the school lodgings were primitive at best, with no heat in the winter, and the food was scanty and poor. Still, the young musician took solace in his lessons, particularly enjoying the evening orchestra rehearsals in which he was able to study the great works of Haydn, Mozart, and his favorite composer, Beethoven. One of his few friends took pity on his poverty, slipping him music paper on which the boy began his prolific composing.

At age sixteen, Schubert's voice broke, which for most chapel boys spelled the end of their careers. Because of his musical talents, Schubert was invited to stay on at the school, but he declined, preferring to return to his home. His father expected him to take up the family business of school teaching. In order to avoid the draft and to please his father, Schubert reluctantly took to the classroom. But his career as an educator would last only two years.

At nineteen, Schubert struck out on his own, gathering around him a crowd of young bohemian artists, singers, and musicians. They spent evenings carousing, enjoying heady discussions, songs, and wine. These companions would be Schubert's lifelong champions: they were the audience for many of his works that were never publically performed, and they supported him through the indifferent reception of his musical output.

Certainly, it was not his physical appearance or his social graces that endeared him to his friends. They nicknamed him "the lump of fat." The pudgy man disdained high society, perhaps because he was terribly shy, and he was indifferent to his clothing and general appearance. One of his confidants said, "To bow or scrape or cringe in society was odious to him, and to be flattered for his genius disgusted him."

By age twenty-three, Schubert had produced a remarkable number of works in all styles, numbering over 500. But only two of these works had been heard on the concert stage. Soon, however, Schubert had commissions from several theaters to write operettas and incidental music for dramatic productions. These works were well received by the public, even while the critics lambasted him for his unusual modern composing style. One critic huffily reported that Schubert's first operetta was "received as a if it were a masterpiece, which, of course, it was not."

The remainder of Schubert's life was marked by lack of public recognition, poverty, and intense suffering from the developing symptoms of syphilis. Still, he was amazingly productive, even as he spent many days unable to eat. It is not surprising that he became increasingly despondent as the illness took its toll on his capabilities. "Picture to yourself," he lamented, "a man whose health can never be re-established . . . whose most brilliant hopes have come to nothing . . . whose enthusiasm for the beautiful threatens to vanish entirely. . . . Each night when I go to sleep I hope never again to waken, and every morning reopens the wounds of yesterday."

It was in the last year of his life that the composer finally was recognized by the Viennese public. An all-Schubert concert was held, and the public packed the hall. The music was enthusiastically received and it seemed that, finally, Schubert's day had come. But, sadly, his life was nearly over, and he soon lapsed into delirium and death.

Little would be known of this master composer today if it were not for the interest of a few devoted friends, music critics, and family members. His brother Ferdinand kept a trunk of manuscripts, which he opened for the famous music critic and composer Robert Schumann ten years after Schubert's death. Among the papers Schumann discovered a gem: the ninth symphony. He championed the work, seeing to its publication and its first performance, under the direction of Felix Mendelssohn.

Other scholars followed in Schumann's footsteps, unearthing what would be recognized as masterpieces of the classical repertoire. In 1865, a conductor decided to produce a program of Viennese music. An old friend of Schubert's possessed yet another trunk of musty manuscripts; among them was the prized "Unfinished" symphony, which was premiered at this concert, nearly fifty years after it was written!

Recommended Listening

Orchestral Works

Schubert composed nine symphonies, the most famous being his "Unfinished" (Symphony No. 8 in B Minor), written when he was twenty-five, and his ninth symphony, written after the so-called "Unfinished" symphony, and so some early writers called it his seventh symphony. Confused yet?

Why the "Unfinished" symphony was never completed is one of those intriguing mysteries of Romantic music. Schubert wrote two complete movements; a third movement exists as a sketch of about 100 measures, and there is no fourth movement at all. Despite the popular notion that Schubert keeled over after completing the first two movements, the composer actually lived six more years and completed another symphony during this period. So, the question remains, why didn't he finish the unfinished symphony?

There are some who believe that the achievement of the first two movements was so great that the composer felt that they stood alone. Of course, if this were the case, why did he begin composing a third movement? Perhaps the composer simply could not equal the inspiration of his opening movements and abandoned the piece as too perfect to be completed.

A symposium held in New York City on Schubert in February

1992 underscored the problems scholars have in interpreting the motivations behind works like the "Unfinished" symphony. In 1989, classical music scholar and record executive Maynard Soloman published a paper asserting that Schubert was gay. This led feminist music scholar Susan McClary to postulate that the "Unfinished" symphony is gay program music. She claims that the tentative longings, unfulfilled assertions, and lingering emotionality are all part of a gay aesthetic. Other music scholars question her findings, saying that we don't know enough about 19th-century Viennese society (let alone 19th-century *gay* society in Vienna) to make these conclusions. So, the "Unfinished" symphony remains as bafflingly "unfinished" as before.

There are many recordings available of the "Unfinished" symphony. Daniel Barenboim conducts the Berlin Philharmonic in this work, along with Schubert's second symphony (Columbia Masterworks MK 39676); Herbert von Karajan conducts the same orchestra performing this work along with the ninth symphony (Deutsche Grammophon 423219-2 GMW). An interesting version is performed by Sir Neville Marriner and the Academy of Saint Martin-in-the-Fields on Philips 412472-2 PH. A reconstruction of the third movement, made by Brian Newbould based on Schubert's 100-measure sketch, is added to the work on this recording.

The ninth symphony, popularly known as "The Great," was the first major work of Schubert's discovered after his death. It combines the magnificence of a Beethoven symphony with the lyricism of Schubert's greatest songs. There are many fine recordings of this work. Sir Georg Solti recorded it leading the Vienna Philharmonic (London 400082-2 LH). George Szell and the Cleveland Orchestra recorded it twice: once in 1957 (Columbia Masterworks MK 42415) along with the "Unfinished" symphony, and again in the 1970s on Columbia Masterworks MYK 37239. The ninth symphony is closely associated with Szell, and his performances are exceptional, particularly the earlier version (even though it is not as good a recording, from a technical point of view, as the later version).

Schubert wrote fifteen string quartets of varying quality. He is best remembered for two of them, the quartets in D minor (popularly known as "Death and the Maiden") and A minor. Both quartets take their melodic inspiration from Schubert's songs. The quartets are great accomplishments in the Classical form, but in emotional tone they belong to the Romantic era. Both have a melancholy that expresses Schubert's world-weary view. The shadow of death that dogged the composer throughout his creative life hovers over these compositions.

For the completist, the Melos Quartet has recorded all of Schubert's quartets on six CDs (Deutsche Grammophon 419879-2 GCM6). The Quartet in A Minor is available on a budget-priced Vox two-CD release by the New Hungarian Quartet, which also features "Death and the Maiden" and two other quartets (Vox Box CDX 5022). The Tokyo String Quartet performs the two quartets on Vox Unique VU 9001, and the Juilliard String Quartet performs them on Odyssey MBK 42602; both of these are budget-priced releases.

Schubert created the piano quintet in his famous work "Die Forelle" or the "Trout Quintet" in A major. It is unusual because it features violin, viola, cello, and double bass, rather than two violins, viola, and cello, as in the normal string quartet; it also has five parts, rather than the normal four. It is based on one of Schubert's popular songs, the light-hearted melody called "Die Forelle." Unlike the string quartets, this is a happy work, marked by joyous melodies drawn from folk traditions. Alfred Brendel and the Cleveland Quartet have recorded it (Philips 400078-2 PH), as have Mieczyslaw Horszowski and the Juilliard String Quartet (along with "Death and the Maiden"; Sony Classical SBK 46343). Peter Serkin performed the work in the early '60s with a special quartet made up for the recording session, including Alexander Schneider on violin (Vanguard Classics OVC 8005).

Piano Works

Schubert was a master improviser on the piano, and his best piano works are short pieces that emulate this offhand, improvised nature. He called some of these brief works "moments musicaux," or musical moments, emotional sketches in musical form. Schubert is most famous for his impromptus, free-ranging improvisations of short duration. Although he did not create this style, he did much to popularize it.

The complete impromptus are available from Daniel Barenboim on Deutsche Grammophon 415849-2 GGA and Alfred Brendel on Philips 422237-2 PH. A selection can be heard by Artur Rubinstein on RCA 6257-2 RC, along with the famed B-flat major piano sonata. Selected piano works can be heard on five CDs (Arabesque Z-6571, 6572, 6573, 6574, 6575) performed by Arthur Schnabel.

In addition to these brief works, Schubert wrote more than twenty piano sonatas. Most of these works have many enchanting moments, but lack a strong unifying structure or coherent development from theme to theme. There are, however, three sonatas written in the last year of his life that transcend all of the others. The Sonata in C Minor opens with an incredible show of force followed by a dramatic heightening of tension through several key changes, reminiscent of Beethoven's confident command of the sonata form. The Sonata in A Major is the ultimate expression of grief over the disappointments that the composer felt in his life. The final sonata, in B-flat major, has an epic cast, with a melodic sweep that only the master songsmith could have fashioned.

The C-minor sonata is available in a recording by Alfred Brendel along with a selection of the musical moments on Philips 422076-2 PH. Murray Perahia has recorded the A-major sonata along with Schumann's Sonata Opus 22 on Columbia Masterworks MK 44569, making for an interesting comparison of the two composers' styles. The B-flat major sonata is the most frequently recorded; some good versions include Vladimir Ashkenazy (London 417327-2 LH) and Vladimir Horowitz (RCA Gold Seal 60451-2-RG).

EIGHT
THE NATIONALISTS

As we've seen, Romanticism inspired a revolution in the way people viewed themselves, their society, and the arts. A new popular audience, drawn from the increasingly wealthy middle class, developed for music, and composers and performers arrived on the scene to meet the demand. An emphasis on the nobility of the common man in Romantic literature and philosophy led to a rediscovery of European folk and national music, and every nook and cranny of Europe seemed to be bursting with musical expression. Collections of traditional (folk) melodies were published by the score, with well-known composers drawing inspiration from them for their works.

The birth of new nations, and the renewed interest in the folklore of the European peoples, led to a new nationalism that found its expression in the work of several prominent composers, themselves coming from among the people. The two most prominent nationalists were Frédéric Chopin and Franz Liszt, one representing his native Poland, the other Hungary. Both were piano virtuosi, and both revolutionized the way the instrument was played and the music that was composed for it. They both came early in the Romantic era, pointing the way for later performers and composers. Later in the century, other national voices were heard, including Antonin Dvořák and Edvard Grieg.

119

Piano Giants

The piano came into its own in the Romantic era, following the great achievements of Beethoven as a performer and composer for the instrument. Improvements in the construction of the instrument and mass marketing meant that by century's end many homes in Europe and the United States had a piano in the front parlor. All of these fledgling pianists needed music to play, and they also made a natural audience for virtuoso performers. Two who early on leapt on the piano bandwagon were Frédéric Chopin and Franz Liszt.

FRÉDÉRIC CHOPIN

b. 1810, Zelazowa Wola, Poland

d. 1849, Paris, France

Chopin was the first composer to make his mark totally as a pianist. While others had composed for the instrument before, he was the first to compose solely for it, and he explored more fully its capabilities than anyone had previously done. His use of harmonies, tonalities, a full dynamic range, and attack and release were so far advanced that it can be truly said that Chopin created the modern piano style.

Chopin was also a uniquely Romantic figure. A Pole by birth, he adapted many Polish folk melodies for his piano works and proudly proclaimed his Polish heritage at a time when Poland was considered the backwater of Europe. In return, the Polish people came to idolize the composer, and his works became symbols of Polish nationalism. When the Nazis invaded Poland in 1939, the last piece played on free Polish radio was a Chopin work, a symbol of national pride and resistance.

Chopin lived the life of a Romantic artist. Slight and shy, he suffered from periods of poor health, leading to his untimely death from tuberculosis at age thirty-nine. A popular figure in Parisian salons, Chopin was ill at ease in large crowds, preferring the rarefied atmosphere of the small private party, where his true personality could shine. Drawn to the wealthy and well-bred, he had a lifelong distaste for poverty, despite his background.

Chopin was born in the small village of Zelazowa Wola to mixed French and Polish parents. His father was a Frenchman who was part of the retinue of the local countess, teaching French to her children. He fell in love with her lady-in-waiting, a Pole of lesser nobility, and they were married. Soon after Frédéric's birth, his father obtained a position as a French teacher at a school in Warsaw, later opening his own small school. So, like Schubert, Chopin came from a humble, but intellectual, background.

From his early years, Chopin showed an interest in the piano, picking out melodies and harmonies. He was such a sensitive child that when one of his self-composed melodies moved him, he would begin to cry. A local fiddler was his first piano teacher, and Frédéric gave his first recital at age nine, followed by many appearances in the homes of Warsaw's nobility. At age fifteen, he entered his father's school and began studying the piano with Joseph Elsner, the director of the Warsaw Conservatory and a sympathetic teacher. Elsner gave him free rein to improvise as he saw fit. Rather than seeking to mold him into a classical musician, Elsner allowed Chopin's natural talents to blossom, encouraging the young composer in the direction of performing and writing in a new style that would become his life's work.

At age eighteen, Chopin made his first trip away from home, to Berlin. This was followed a year later by a trip to Vienna, where he gave two acclaimed concerts and published his first work. An unhappy love affair at home, plus his realization that there was a world beyond Warsaw, led Chopin to leave his hometown permanently in 1830. Elsner presented him with a silver container filled with Polish earth: "May you never forget your native land wherever you may go," he advised his pupil. Chopin remained true to these wishes; the vial of Polish earth was buried with him nineteen years later.

Chopin first traveled to Vienna, where news of the Polish uprising against Russian rule reached him. He hired a coach to return home to join the fight, but second thoughts dogged him and, realizing that his true genius lay off the battlefield, he returned to Vienna. From there he traveled to Paris, with the ultimate goal of reaching London. Instead, Paris became his home for the rest of his life.

Chopin's first concerts in Paris were not successful. His playing was too intimate for French ears, and his works not grand enough to move a large audience. Discouraged, the composer began to make plans to travel to America. As luck would have it, he gained an introduction to the burgeoning French salon society, led by wealthy middle-class bankers and businessmen who were becoming important patrons of the arts. In the small salons, Chopin's unique piano playing was instantly recognized as an important breakthrough, and soon he was in demand at all of the fashionable homes. Publishers vied for the rights to print his works, and he was flooded with offers to teach his new technique to the leisured classes.

Chopin began to compose the pieces that would make him famous: short piano studies in the forms of nocturnes, polonaises, waltzes, études, and mazurkas. These free-form, brief works were admired for their jewel-like construction, the beauty and sentiment of their melodies, and their fragility and charm. Chopin discovered that he could be "great in small things," as one contemporary critic wrote. The age of intimate music was born.

In the fashionable salons, Chopin met the love of his life: the French author and intellectual George Sand. Sand wrote novels under a man's name, dressed in masculine clothes, and smoked cigars! A deep thinker, she was celebrated as much for her shocking affairs and her illegitimate birth as she was for her literary output. Chopin, an effeminate, frail man, was at first put off by Sand, who was hardly a classical beauty. But it seems their personalities complemented each other, and they had a stormy relationship from their meeting in 1837 until shortly before the composer's death.

Already ailing in 1838, Chopin followed Sand to her summer home for some much-needed care. In 1839, the two made an ill-fated trip to Majorca, looking for a spot where they could live together freely and Chopin's health problems could improve. Sadly, the locals were even more close-minded than Parisian society, frowning on the scandalous behavior of this couple who refused to attend church and lived together although they were not married. Moreover, the weather conspired against them, turning wet and cold, so that Chopin suffered from several severe lung hemorrhages and nearly died.

On returning to France, Chopin rallied briefly, producing some of his most famous works and enjoying his greatest popularity as a performer. This period came to an end in 1841, when the efforts of composing and performing led to a final breakdown in his health. Although he lived another eight years, he performed only occasionally. In 1848, he ended his difficult relationship with Sand, who had apparently tired of playing nursemaid to the perpetually ailing composer. Liszt commented: "Chopin often repeated that in breaking this long affection, this powerful bond, he had broken his life."

Although he retained a few friends in the salons who supported him in his time of illness, Chopin was indeed a broken man. He made one final trip, reaching England and Scotland, but the damp English weather aggravated his condition. On returning to Paris, he withdrew into his apartment and silence. He died in October of 1849.

Recommended Listening

Chopin produced two orchestral works which, not surprisingly, took the form of piano concerti. Both were written early in his career, just before he left Poland, and were premiered there by the composer. The Concerto No. 1 in E Minor is the more famous of the pair; although premiered first, it was actually written second, after the Concerto No. 2 in F Minor. Considering that these works were composed when Chopin was only nineteen, they are remarkable for their depth of feeling. Although some critics complain that he was not a master of longer forms like the concerto, it is perhaps wiser to view these pieces as Romantic reveries, freeform works that perfectly capture the spirit of Romanticism. In fact, Chopin called the second movement of the E-minor work "Romanza," and he explained that the work was "intended to convey the impression which one receives when the eye rests on a beloved landscape that calls up in one's soul beautiful memories—for instance, on a fine moonlit spring night."

These oft-recorded works are available in performances by

Claudio Arrau and the Philadelphia Orchestra under the baton of Eugene Ormandy (RCA RCD1-5317), Murray Perahia and the Israel Philharmonic Orchestra directed by Zubin Mehta (Sony Classical SK 44992), André Watts with the New York Philharmonic Orchestra under the lead of Thomas Schippers (Sony Classical SBK 46336), and Artur Rubinstein with the New Symphony of London (RCA 5612-2-RC).

Chopin created an extensive library of solo piano works, encompassing a remarkable range of emotions. The legendary pianist Artur Rubinstein described the Chopin oeuvre in these words: "Tragic, romantic, lyric, heroic, dramatic, fantastic, soulful, sweet, dreamy, brilliant, grand, simple: all possible expressions are found in his compositions, and all are sung by him upon his instrument."

Chopin was not too successful writing in larger forms such as the sonata. Robert Schumann complained that his sonatas were little more than four independent works arbitrarily put together: "He has simply linked together four of his maddest children in order to introduce them under this name into a place which otherwise they would perhaps never have entered." Still, the sonatas contain many breathtaking moments and famous melodies, such as the celebrated funeral march found in the second piano sonata. The Sonata No. 2 in B Minor is the most frequently recorded of these works, and is available in performances by Vladimir Horowitz (RCA Gold Seal 60376-2-RG), Abbey Simon (Vox Unique VU 9032), Vladimir Ashkenazy (London 41779-2 LM), and Emanuel Ax (RCA Silver Seal 60480-2-RV), to name a few.

Chopin was celebrated for his nocturnes, short, dreamy pieces that expressed perfectly the Romantic languor of a Viennese night. The nocturne form was not invented by Chopin; this honor falls to the Irish-born pianist John Field, who performed some of his own nocturnes at a concert in Paris in 1832 that the Polish composer attended. Soon after, Chopin was writing his own nocturnes, deeper and more expressive than those played by Field.

Among Chopin's first nocturnes is the famous work in E-flat major, which has been transcribed for violin and piano and for cello and piano. Also noteworthy is the A-flat major nocturne, adapted for use as one of the main themes in the ballet *Les Sylphides*. Claudio Arrau has recorded the complete nocturnes on a two-CD set (Philips 416440-2 PH2), as have Daniel Barenboim (Deutsche Grammophon 423916-2 GGA2), Ivan Moravec (Nonesuch 79233-2, a budget-priced recording), and Artur Rubinstein (RCA 5613-2-RC).

Chopin composed twenty-four études, or piano studies, published in two volumes. These exercises allowed the composer to explore various aspects of piano technique. But, typically for this composer, they are not mere studies; they have a lyricism rarely found in the form. The so-called "Revolutionary" étude is one of the most famous, inspired by the uprising against Russian rule in Chopin's native Poland. Chopin also composed twenty-six preludes, or short pieces capturing a specific mood. Before Chopin, preludes were written to introduce a fugue or other work; Chopin made the work stand alone as its own Romantic tone poem. One of the most famous of these works is the "Raindrop," so called because of the pitter-pattering rhythm in the bass, suggesting the sound of rain falling on a rooftop. Abbey Simon has recorded the complete études as part of his budget-priced complete Chopin on Vox (VU 9033). Another collection of the complete études is by Claudio Arrau (Angel CDH-61016). Maurizio Pollini recorded the études along with Chopin's polonaises and preludes on a three-CD set (Deutsche Grammophon 43122102 GX3).

Chopin's waltzes were inspired by the success of Johann Strauss, the so-called "Waltz King," whose "On the Beautiful Blue Danube" has been a perennial favorite. But Chopin refined the form, taking it away from the dance hall into the rarefied atmosphere of the salon. One of his most famous works in this form is the "Minute Waltz," named because of its finely crafted form (from the French "minute," meaning of short duration; it actually takes about three minutes to perform.) Chopin's waltzes have been recorded by Alexander Brailowsky (Sony Classical SBK 46346), Vladimir Ashkenazy (London 414600-2 LH), Dinu Lipatti (Angel CDC 47390), and Abbey Simon (Vox Unique VU 9034).

Finally, in his polonaises and mazurkas, Chopin drew on his Polish roots to create music that is at once noble and stridently national. The polonaise, a dance in triple meter, has a definite grandiose personality. Chopin's works in this form breathe fire, pomp, and glory. Select polonaises have been recorded by Alfred

Brendel (Vanguard Classics OVC 4023) and Vladimir Horowitz (Columbia Masterworks MK-42412), along with other works. The mazurka is a slow piece in 3/4 (waltz) time, but the accent comes on the last beat rather than the first, as in the waltz. These pieces are more contemplative, freer in form, and reflect a wider variety of emotions than the polonaises. Jan Ekeir has recorded the complete mazurkas on a two-CD set (Muza PNCD 056 A + B), as has Artur Rubinstein (RCA 5614-2-RC).

There are many sampler CDs available giving an overview of Chopin's most popular piano works. Vladimir Horowitz is considered to have been one of this century's finest interpreters of Chopin; a good selection of his recordings is available on *Favorite Chopin* (Columbia Masterworks MK 42306). Other able interpreters include Van Cliburn (*My Favorite Chopin*; RCA Gold Seal 60358-2-RG), Malcolm Frager (*Plays Chopin*; Telarc CD-80280), Peter Serkin (Pro Arte CDD 246), and historic recordings by Ignatz Jan Paderewski (Pearl GEMM CD 9397).

FRANZ LISZT

  b. 1811, Raiding, Hungary
  d. 1886, Bayreuth, Bavaria

Liszt's life story is in many ways reminiscent of Chopin's. He, too, was an Eastern European who became an international symbol of his nation's culture. He was a child prodigy on the piano and performed widely as a young musician. However, unlike Chopin, Liszt cut a dashing figure in society and on the stage, and truly can be called the first great showman, enacting the emotions that he played and sometimes swooning or wiping away a tear as the feelings moved him. Leading a life that vacillated between periods of piety and debauchery, Liszt was the ultimate "Romantic" figure on the Romantic stage.

Liszt's father was an amateur musician in the employment of the duke of Esterházy, the same family that had supported Haydn. At the age of nine, Franz Liszt was already able to play complex works on the piano expertly and to improvise on a theme. This so impressed Esterházy that he and his friends raised enough money for the young man's musical education. The family relocated to

Vienna, where the prodigy studied piano with Karl Czerny and composition with Antonio Salieri. At one performance, Beethoven lifted young Liszt in his arms and kissed him, pronouncing him a musical genius.

At the age of twelve, Liszt traveled to Paris to study in the Conservatory only to discover that foreigners were not admitted to the school, no matter how talented. He soon was taking private lessons, performing widely, and composing his first large-scale work, the opera *Don Sanche*, which is today thankfully forgotten. In 1827 his father died, happy that his son was so widely successful but worried already that his effect on women would prove unsettling to his career. The dashing young man was winning hearts at an alarming rate, and his musical development was threatened by his emotional entanglements.

His father's death led Liszt to vow to turn over a new leaf: he would give up being a mere performer and plaything of the wealthy and turn his attention to true musical achievement. He also vowed to turn his back on petty romances. He seems to have kept the first vow, as he disappeared from the concert stage. But the later vow was shattered by a pretty, sixteen-year-old noblewoman. However, her father ended the budding affair, leading to a period of depression for Liszt, followed by a sudden interest in religion. Religion gave way to politics, which gave way to his first love, music, spurred on by his meeting in 1830 with three key figures: Hector Berlioz, Frédéric Chopin, and particularly Niccolò Paganini.

Berlioz and Chopin were both budding composers, but each had something to offer to Liszt. Chopin's exquisite new style of playing the piano and his brilliantly crafted concert pieces pointed the way to a new manner of composing. Berlioz was more experimental, pushing forward the traditions of piano playing, and his masculine vitality at the keyboard became a key ingredient in Liszt's work. But it was Paganini—the fiery violinist who seemed to draw blood from the strings—who had the most profound influence. Liszt vowed to become the Paganini of the piano, and indeed, his return to the concert stage three years later announced a new level of showmanship never before seen.

Liszt's new-found passion was mirrored in his private life. He was conducting a steamy affair with the Countess d'Agoult, who was high-born, beautiful, smart, and most importantly, infatuated with the Hungarian. The fact that she was already married was not an impediment; soon the two were living together in Geneva, and the Countess bore three of Liszt's many illegitimate children, including a daughter, Cosima, who would later marry the composer Richard Wagner.

Liszt ruled the concert stage as no one had before. One contemporary description aptly captures the Lisztian style, one part Little Richard, one part Madonna, one part Prince (all of whom could learn some moves from the elder musician): "As the closing strains began I saw Liszt's countenance assume that agony of expression, mingled with radiant smiles of joy, which I never saw in any other human face. . . . He fainted in the arms of a friend who was turning over the pages for him and we bore him out in a strong fit of hysterics. . . . The whole room sat breathless with fear, till Hiller [Liszt's friend] came forward and announced that Liszt was already restored to consciousness and was comparatively well again."

Liszt took full advantage of his appearance to win over the crowd. He kept his hair long and would throw his head back so that it would fall from his face in a thrilling gesture. He recognized that his profile was his strongest asset; women swooned when they saw him. For this reason, he insisted that the piano be turned so that his profile would be visible to the audience. This innovation has come down to our day, so that all pianists insist on a profile position (the pianist faced the audience in the old days, so that neither his hands, body gestures, or face could be seen).

Liszt's love life continued on its up-and-down rollercoaster ride. He had abandoned the Countess d'Agoult by 1844, but three years later he had a new admirer, the eccentric Princess Carolyne von Sayn-Wittgenstein of Kiev. An intelligent woman interested in mysticism, the Princess smoked cigars and had an unnatural fear of fresh air, insisting that her rooms be carefully sealed and that visitors spend a fifteen-minute "de-ventilating" period in an antechamber before being admitted into her specially designed apartment. She was a night owl, working many hours on a projected twenty-four-volume analysis of the failures of organized religion.

Despite these eccentricities, the Princess joined Liszt when he began a ten-year appointment as kapellmeister to the Grand Duke of Weimar. During this period of his life, Liszt served an important role as champion of younger composers, vowing to make Weimar the musical center of Europe. He befriended many composers, particularly the young Richard Wagner, whom he pronounced a genius. Liszt was to remain an important figure in the younger composer's professional and personal life, although he was angered when Wagner took an interest in his illegitimate daughter, Cosima, who was already married to someone else. Their love affair led to the breakup of her marriage and an estrangement with her father that lasted for some time.

The Weimar audience became increasingly confused by the ultramodern works that Liszt was presenting. Eventually, they forced his retirement as kapellmeister. He spent the rest of his life in vain pursuit of a position in the church. It was, naturally, difficult for such a famous showman and womanizer to be given a significant church appointment. Meanwhile, he gave piano lessons, influencing an entire generation of performers. He also played an important role in the founding of the Bayreuth Festival, a musical event championed by Wagner that drew composers, performers, and an audience from throughout Europe. It was at this festival in 1886 that Liszt took ill during a performance of Wagner's opera *Tristan und Isolde*. Pneumonia set in and the composer soon died, his last words being the name of the Romantic hero Tristan.

Recommended Listening

Although Liszt lived a long and active life, his musical legacy is smaller than the shorter-lived Chopin or Schubert. Ultimately, his musical achievement was not terribly great, although he did bequeath two new forms to Romantic music: the symphonic tone poem, an impressionistic work that musically describes an abstract mood or feeling, and the famous piano rhapsodies, works of high emotion noted for their quick changes in tempo and mood. Liszt's orchestral works are not favorites in the repertoire today. The tone poems, while revolutionary at the time of their composition, are not often revived. The third symphonic poem, called

"Les Preludes," is the only one of the twelve that is played with any regularity. The work describes the life of man, from puppy love through trials and tribulations in the real world of work and war to final self-recognition. The work has been recorded by Leonard Bernstein and the New York Philharmonic (Columbia Masterworks MYK 37772), a recording that also features the famous orchestration of Liszt's Hungarian Rhapsody No. 2. Sir Georg Solti also recorded "Les Preludes," along with three more of the tone poems, with the London Philharmonic Orchestra (London 417513-2).

Of Liszt's other orchestral works, the most often performed is his Concerto for Piano and Orchestra in E-flat Major. It was not well received on its first performance: a critic sarcastically called it "the triangle concerto," because of Liszt's prominent use of this instrument that is not often featured in an orchestral work. The nickname has stuck, although it is no longer used derisively. The piece was revived in the mid-19th century and has since become a staple of the concert repertoire for pianists who really want to show their chops! The work is unusual in that there are no breaks between the movements; instead, Liszt used certain repeated melodic themes as a way of unifying it, foreshadowing the use of leitmotifs by Wagner. Liszt wrote one other piano concerto, in A major. The two works are available in many recordings, including Misha Dichter with the Pittsburgh Symphony under the direction of André Previn (Philips 420896-2 PM) and Alfred Brendel performing with Michael Gielen conducting the Vienna Symphony Orchestra (Preiser 90064).

It is as a pianist that Liszt made his mark, particularly with his "Hungarian Rhapsodies." Enchanted by his native land's traditional music, Liszt published ten volumes of Hungarian folk melodies between 1839 and 1847. In 1851, he composed his first Hungarian rhapsody based on these traditional dance tunes, and he continued to compose them until 1854. Liszt made masterful use of the unusual rhythms and minor tonalities of Hungarian traditional music, and the rhapsodies are marked by dramatic swings in mood from joyous to solemn, from funereal to dancing, from sentimental to deeply emotive. The Hungarian Rhapsody No. 2 is famous today in its orchestrated version and was used to great comic effect in Charlie Chaplin's *The Great Dictator*, in which a barber shaves a customer to its strains.

The "Hungarian Rhapsodies" are available in their original piano versions and in orchestral transcriptions (some of which were made by Liszt himself). Alfred Brendel has recorded a good selection of them on piano (Vanguard Classics OVC 4024). Of the orchestrated versions, Herbert von Karajan with the Berlin Philharmonic (Deutsche Grammophon 419862-2 GGA) presents two of the more popular rhapsodies, along with the tone poem "Mephisto Waltz"; CBS Masterworks MYK-37772 features Leonard Bernstein and the New York Philharmonic performing the Rhapsody No. 1 and Eugene Ormandy and the Philadelphia Orchestra performing Rhapsody No. 2.

There are numerous CDs that give an overview of Liszt's piano music, including recordings by Claudio Arrau (Ermitage ERM 104), Vladimir Horowitz (RCA Gold Seal 60523-2-RG), Murray Perahia (Sony Classical SK 46437), and André Watts (Angel CDC-47380, 47381). An interesting CD is Jeno Jando's *The Instruments of Liszt*, featuring performances on seven pianos that Liszt actually owned and played (Hungaroton HCD-31176). For an overview of Liszt's entire repertoire, Columbia Masterworks checks in with *Liszt's Greatest Hits* (MLK-39450) and Allegretto with *Lots of Liszt* (ACD 88718).

Other National Voices

There were many composers who came out of the far corners of Europe who were influential in the growth of 19th-century Romanticism. Antonin Dvořák, a Czech, and Edvard Grieg, a Scottish-descended Norwegian, were two of the most important.

ANTONIN DVOŘÁK

b. 1841, Muhlhausen, Bohemia (Czechoslovakia)

d. 1904, Prague, Czechoslovakia

Dvořák was truly a folk composer, coming from an impoverished background. His father was a butcher and innkeeper and also an amateur musician, playing the violin and zither. Music was a central part of the folk life of the Bohemians; Dvořák himself said: "Every child must learn music and if possible sing in the church. After church the people revel in music and dancing, sometimes until early morning." The young Dvořák was soon fiddling at local fairs, hearing gypsy bands, and absorbing traditional folk tunes.

His father hoped his son would become an innkeeper, not a musician, and for this purpose sent him, at age fourteen, to his brother's home to learn German, an all-purpose language for a hostler. There Dvořák met Antonin Liehmann, a music teacher who taught him viola, piano, and organ. Liehmann urged the elder Dvořák to send his son to Prague to study, but the father viewed music as an avocation at best, not an occupation, and refused to allow him to continue his training. The friction between father and son smoldered until Dvořák's sixteenth birthday, when he set out on his own.

His ascent to musical fame was a rocky one. He spent eleven years as an underpaid member of the National Opera Orchestra in Prague, where he was engaged in "hard study, occasional composing, much revision, a great deal of thinking, and very little eating," in his own words. Dvořák had the opportunity to hear the work of the Opera's conductor, Bedrich Smetana, who was an important early composer in the national style.

At the age of thirty-two, Dvořák retired from the orchestra to become a church organist, marrying one of his music students. To support himself, "I ate less and gave more lessons," Dvořák said. He also struggled toward his mature style. While his early works had been derivative of the great German composers, Smetana pointed the way to a new style, culled from Bohemia's own music. His first success in this new style was the orchestral work "The Heirs of the White Mountain."

Another Bohemian-influenced work, "Airs from Moravia," won him a small pension from the Austrian government. One member of the adjudicating panel was Johannes Brahms, who became Dvořák's lifelong friend and champion. Brahms promoted the composer's work in Vienna, arranged for publication of his compositions, and helped him edit and refine his compositions. Brahms arranged for a commission for the composer from his publisher to write a series of "Slavonic Dances" in the manner of Brahms's earlier "Hungarian Dances." These were an immediate sensation, establishing a Europe-wide audience for the composer.

In 1884, he was invited to perform in London and was immediately hailed as a success. One year later he was hired to be a teacher at a new music school in New York, the National Conservatory of Music, established by a wealthy socialite. Dvořák remained in New York for three years and became deeply interested in African-American and Native American music. He used many African-American musical themes in his famous symphony "From the New World" and urged other American composers to draw on traditional material for their inspiration. The symphony was premiered in 1893 by the New York Philharmonic and was an immediate success.

In 1895, Dvořák returned to his beloved Prague, and six years later he was appointed head of the music conservatory. His last years were marred by the failure of his opera *Armida*. Soon after its disastrous premiere, the composer died of a massive stroke.

Recommended Listening

Dvořák's best-known work is the symphony "From the New World," his ninth symphony (a magic number in classical music). It incorporates many beloved folk melodies, including "Swing Low, Sweet Chariot," as filtered through the composer's unique vision. It is said that because Dvořák came from such modest beginnings, he had a special feeling for folk melodies. "From the New World" inspired other composers to look toward their national origins for inspiration and helped elevate the artistry of African-Americans, whose music found a strong new champion.

There are many recordings of this work, including Leonard Bernstein with the Israel Philharmonic (Deutsche Grammophon 427346-2 GH), Arthur Fiedler and the Boston Pops (RCA Papillon Collection 6530-2-RG), Herbert von Karajan (who recorded it four times; one version is on Deutsche Grammophon 415509-2 GH), and Eugene Ormandy and the Philadelphia Orchestra (RCA Silver Seal 60537-2-RV).

The "Slavonic Dances" have also been widely recorded, both as piano duets and in orchestrations. Ingryd Thorson and Julian

Thurber have recorded these works on two pianos (Olympia OCD 362); Kurt Masur with the Leipzig Gewandhaus Orchestra (Philips 416623-2 PH) give a good orchestral reading.

One of Dvořák's most famous piano works is "Humoresque," composed in 1895 on his return to Czechoslovakia. Actually, Dvořák wrote a series of playful piano pieces that he labeled as a group "Humoresques," but only one has survived in the popular repertoire as the "Humoresque." Fritz Kreisler, the famous violinist, transcribed it for his instrument, and it became a part of every virtuoso's repertoire. One of the more unusual interpretations came from Zez Confrey, the famous ragtime orchestra leader and pianist who composed "Kitten on the Keys," who wrote a jazz-influenced parody of the piece that he called "Humor-restless." The entire group of eight pieces has been recorded by Radoslav Kvapil on Supraphonet 11 1113-2.

EDVARD GRIEG

b. 1843, Bergen, Norway
d. 1907, Bergen, Norway

Grieg did for Norwegian music what Dvořák did for Bohemian music: he put it on the map. One contemporary critic called Grieg "the Chopin of the North," and the two musicians shared many characteristics: both were excellent composers for the piano, both excelled at small, finely crafted works, and both drew on their native traditions to create music of deep national feeling.

Grieg came from middle-class stock, and his parents were talented amateur musicians, particularly his mother, who was a fine pianist. Somewhat of an undirected youth, Grieg had difficulties in school and could not seem to focus on his studies. He showed an early talent at the keyboards, effortlessly picking out melodies and harmonies and composing his first work in the Germanic manner at the age of twelve. This so impressed a family friend, the noted violinist Ole Bull, that he urged Grieg's parents to send the young man to a conservatory in Leipzig.

Music school turned out to be just as trying for Grieg as regular school. He could not focus on the academic studies that were foisted on him and found his teachers' old-fashioned attitudes annoying. They regularly pooh-poohed the works of Chopin, who had become the young man's favorite composer. He found writing in the German style ultimately unsatisfying, even though his compositions met with some success.

At age twenty, Grieg returned to his homeland, still in search of a musical style. One year later he befriended Rikard Nordraak, a young composer who would go on to write the Norwegian national anthem. A strident nationalist, Nordraak introduced Grieg to Norwegian folk melodies and converted him to the beauties of his country's music. The two vowed to become champions of Norwegian composers and formed a Norwegian music society. Sadly, Nordraak died two years later, but his death inspired Grieg to pursue further his goal of becoming a spokesman for his native land. He arranged for a concert, in memory of Nordraak, of Norwegian composers, including himself, the first all-Norwegian program ever performed. The public was enthusiastic, and this success led to Grieg's first period of relative fame. He was invited to conduct the prestigious Philharmonic Society Orchestra, his piano recitals were enthusiastically received and well attended, and his list of pupils grew.

In 1869, he was contacted by Franz Liszt, who admired the Norwegian's work. Grieg went to Italy to visit Liszt, and the two became fast friends. Liszt's honest criticism of Grieg's work inspired him to compose his Concerto in A Minor for Piano and Orchestra, still one of his most popular works. Liszt worked tirelessly to urge others to perform Grieg's music and pressed his publisher to accept Grieg's works.

By the mid-1870s, Grieg was well established in his homeland as an important composer. The government provided him with a small subsidy that enabled him to concentrate his energies on composing. In 1876, the famous Scandinavian playwright Henrik Ibsen invited him to write incidental music for his new play, *Peer Gynt*. The music, arranged in two suites, was an immediate hit throughout Europe and has outlived the play in popularity.

From that point on, Grieg enjoyed a life of wide acclaim as a composer and musical mentor. He built a large villa six miles outside of his native Bergen. His music studio was built on the edge of a fjord; a small shack was constructed on a rock overhanging the water and equipped with a piano and desk. Here, in his natural element, he composed. So many people loved him that visitors overran his estate; in desperation, he posted a sign that stated "Edvard Grieg does not desire to receive callers earlier than four in the afternoon."

Grieg's life ended with great acclaim. He was given numerous degrees and awards. Although he requested a simple funeral, over 400,000 people lined the streets of Bergen to salute his casket.

Recommended Listening

Grieg is best remembered today for two orchestral works: the Concerto for Piano and Orchestra in A Minor and the so-called "Peer Gynt Suite." The concerto contains many well-known melodies that have been borrowed by pop songwriters over the years. It is also heard in the popular Broadway musical *Song of Norway*. Kjell Boekkelund performing with the Oslo Philharmonic Orchestra under the direction of Odd Grüner-Hegge can be heard performing this work, along with both "Peer Gynt" suites, on the budget-priced RCA Silver Seal 60538-2-RV. Van Cliburn recorded the concerto with the Philadelphia Orchestra directed by Eugene Ormandy (RCA 7834-2-RG), along with Liszt's two piano concerti, and Murray Perahia with Colin Davis leading the Bavarian Symphony Orchestra plays it, along with Schumann's piano concerto (Columbia Masterworks MK-44899).

The "Peer Gynt Suite" is actually two suites; the first is the more famous. Although this work solidified Grieg's fame, he was hesitant to take on the job when Ibsen first approached him. He did not think the allegorical drama that Ibsen wrote was a natural for musical accompaniment, and he slaved for two years over music that, at the end, he felt did not adequately capture Ibsen's vision. It must have been a pleasant surprise when the work was universally acclaimed. One of the most famous of the melodies in the suites is "In the Hall of the Mountain King," featured in the first suite.

Leonard Bernstein recorded the first "Peer Gynt Suite" with the New York Philharmonic Orchestra (Columbia Masterworks MYK-36718), along with Jean Sibelius's "Finlandia," as did Herbert von Karajan (Deutsche Grammophon 410026-2 GH), along with another Sibelius work, "Pelléas et Mélisande."

NINE
ROMANTIC POTPOURRI

The Romantic movement spawned many great symphonists, composers of large-scale works that remain staples of the concert repertoire. In this chapter, we'll take a look at four of the giants of the Romantic school: Felix Mendelssohn, Gustav Mahler, Johannes Brahms, and Piotr Ilyich Tchaikovsky. Although they share a common heritage, each represents a different facet of the Romantic achievement.

FELIX MENDELSSOHN

b. 1809, Hamburg, Germany

d. 1847, Leipzig, Germany

Romantic composers (a) are born to poverty; (b) struggle with their parents, who do not support them in their musical careers; (c) fight an endless uphill battle with critics and their audience for acceptance; (d) are unlucky in love, loving too many too well; (e) die young of mysterious causes. Felix Mendelssohn was (a) born to wealth and position; (b) had supportive parents who nurtured his musical career; (c) found ready acceptance among the public and critics from his first performance; (d) loved one woman his entire life; (e) died young . . . but died happy! Can this be the life story of a Romantic composer?

The story of the Mendelssohn family combines vast intellect with business acumen. The founding patriarch of the clan was Moses Mendelssohn, Felix's grandfather. He was born an itinerant peddler, a deformed hunchback who subsisted on the lowest rung of the social ladder. Who would have predicted that such a lowly man would become universally applauded as "another Plato," addressing vast metaphysical questions such as the immortality of the soul? Thinkers as great as Immanuel Kant freely acknowledged their debt to his writings.

Moses's son was no intellectual fireball, but he did inherit his father's business acumen. Building on a small legacy, the younger Mendelssohn became a wealthy banker. His wife was an attractive catch, not only a beauty but a great intellect, noted for her command of linguistics (she read the ancient classics in the original Greek!) and her skillful painting and piano playing.

It is natural in such a household that the children would be exposed to the arts. Felix and his sister Fanny were both trained at the keyboard from an early age, and each showed unusual talents. Felix was the most talented, picking out melodies as if from thin air, showing a remarkable ability to memorize works on sight, improvising freely, and easily harmonizing his own creations. He made his concert debut at age nine; by age twelve, he was composing everything from symphonies to operas, showing a mature understanding of each form.

A crisis came to the Mendelssohn family when the ten-year-old Felix was invited to join the Singakademie, the most famous boys' choir in Germany. Choral music at this time was largely religious, and there were some choristers who openly mocked the idea of a young Jewish boy singing the sacred music of the Protestant church. Already exposed to anti-Semitism in his banking business, the elder Mendelssohn decided the family should convert to Protestantism to smooth the young man's progress in the musical world. The family affixed the name Bartholdy to their surname to distinguish themselves from their Jewish relatives.

Mendelssohn's teen years were ones of continued triumphs. The Mendelssohn home was a center of musical activity. As patrons of the arts, the Mendelssohns were visited by many of the leading composers and performers of the day, and the young man had a chance to perform for and learn from them. When he was twelve years old, his teacher took him to Weimar to meet the famous German poet Goethe, sixty years his senior. Goethe was immediately taken with the young musician's prodigious abilities, and he invited him to visit him whenever he was in Weimar. The elder poet pronounced him another Mozart; Goethe was in a unique position to judge, because he was one of the few living Germans who had heard Mozart perform. No doubt some of Mendelssohn's success can be attributed to his unusual good looks and his sophisticated manners. But still, the music came first; by seventeen, he had already produced one of his classic works, the first version of the overture to *A Midsummer Night's Dream*.

Mendelssohn's early twenties were spent in two important endeavors: reviving interest in the music of Bach, whom his mother had greatly admired, and traveling throughout Europe to perform Bach's music. Mendelssohn revived Bach's "St. Matthew Passion" in a performance in 1829; this was the first important presentation of a work by Bach in modern Germany, and it launched the first Bach revival. Shortly after this performance, he began a European tour, making his first trip to England, where he was received enthusiastically. England would become a second home to the composer, inspiring many of his works.

In the mid-1830s, Mendelssohn served as musical director to the courts at Dusseldorf and Leipzig, holding the latter post for five years. He was happy in Leipzig, befriending many important musicians, including Robert and Clara Schumann. His happiness was dampened by the news of his father's death in 1835, but this was balanced by his successful courtship of the seventeen-year-old daughter of a well-to-do Frankfurt family, Cecile Jeanrenaud. The two were married in 1837.

Mendelssohn's Leipzig years were interrupted in the early 1840s when the King of Prussia requested that he travel to Berlin to head the music department of an arts school that the King hoped to establish. Unable to turn down a king, Mendelssohn reluctantly moved to Berlin, returning to Leipzig in 1842 to premiere his famous "Scotch" symphony. Soon after, the Berlin school project collapsed and the King gave Mendelssohn the honorary title of kapellmeister. He could return to his beloved Leipzig, although he would be required to compose music for the King's entertainment. It was in this capacity that he completed his music for *A Midsummer Night's Dream*, including the famous wedding march.

In 1843, Mendelssohn achieved his dream of opening a conservatory of music in Leipzig. With the King's blessing, he hired some of the great musicians of his day to teach there, and he taught piano. Although he was wholeheartedly devoted to the school, Mendelssohn maintained a rigorous schedule of performing and traveling, and his health began to suffer. In 1847, news of the death of his beloved sister shocked him so greatly that he fainted and fell, breaking a blood vessel in his head. Although he recovered from the blow, he was never again himself, suddenly lacking all enthusiasm for life. He died six months later.

Mendelssohn was memorialized in concerts from London to Paris to Italy to every major German city. It was a unique testimony to the impact of this one musician on the course of Romantic music.

Recommended Listening

Orchestral Works

Mendelssohn's best-known symphonies are his third (known as the "Scotch" symphony) and fourth (known as the "Italian" symphony). The numbering of these works is somewhat confusing, since the fourth was actually composed before the third. As in many cases in the history of music, the numbering of the works refers to the order in which they were published, not composed. To make matters more confusing, the young Mendelssohn composed twelve symphonies for string orchestra that aren't counted; his so-called "first" symphony was really his thirteenth symphonic work chronologically, but the first scored for a full orchestra.

The A minor, or "Scotch," symphony was inspired by Mendelssohn's trip to Scotland when he was twenty years old. Written some twelve years later, the work conjures up a Scottish landscape, alternating a melancholic, misty mood with the lilting melodies of the dance music of Scotland. The "Italian" symphony was inspired by a trip to Italy in 1830, following Mendelssohn's stay in Scotland. It was completed two years later. Its buoyant, youthful nature reflects Mendelssohn's enthusiasm for the Italian countryside; he incorporated into its final movement Italian dance forms as an homage to these most musical people.

Both of these symphonies have been recorded by most of today's leading orchestras, and they are often packaged together on a single CD. A few noteworthy interpretations come from Claudio Abbado and the London Symphony on Deutsche Grammophon 427810-2 GDC (also released on London 425011-2 LM), Kurt Masur and the Leipzig Gewandhaus Orchestra on Teldec 43676 ZK, and Sir Georg Solti with the Chicago Symphony Orchestra on London 414655-2 LH.

Mendelssohn contributed one concerto that has become a staple of the classical repertoire. The Concerto in E Minor for Violin and Orchestra is the ideal marriage of Classical form with Romantic feeling. The work has three parts, but Mendelssohn specified that there be no pause between them, so that the mood could be properly maintained throughout the work. The beautiful opening violin solo comes just one measure into the work; it is one of Mendelssohn's most lyrical themes. Pinchas Zukerman conducts and takes the solo chair in a fine recording with the St. Paul Chamber Orchestra on Philips 412212-2 PH. Nadja Salerno-Sonnenberg has recorded this work with the New York Symphony on Angel CDC-49276, pairing it with Saint-Saëns's "Havanaise," and Itzhak Perlman has given an equally Romantic reading to this work with the Royal Concertgebouw Orchestra of Amsterdam under the baton of Bernard Haitink (Angel CDEC-49486).

One of Mendelssohn's best-loved orchestral works is the incidental music composed for *A Midsummer Night's Dream*. The overture was written when he was only seventeen, but it remains one of the great achievements of Romantic music. It perfectly captures the mood of Shakespeare's play, from the impish Puck to the majesty of the Fairy Queen to the buffoonery of Nick Bottom, the weaver who is transformed into an ass. Of the remaining music, the "Wedding March" is the most popular. More women and men have stepped down the aisle to their fate to these notes than to any other composition, with the possible exception of "Here Comes the Bride." The complete work is available in a performance by the Vienna Philharmonic Orchestra and Vienna

Jeunesse Choir under the direction of André Previn (Philips 420161-2 PH). Most listeners would prefer selections rather than the entire work: some good offerings come from the Boston Symphony Orchestra (Philips 420653-2 PH) and George Szell and the Cleveland Orchestra (Columbia Masterworks MYK 37760). Both of these recordings also feature the fourth symphony.

Piano Music

The "Songs Without Words" are Mendelssohn's most important contributions to piano literature. Totaling forty-eight brief works, these are lyrical fragments that express deep emotions without an accompanying text. Mendelssohn was able to capture a wide variety of moods in these pieces; the most famous include the "Funeral March," "Hunting Song," descriptive "Venetian Boat Songs," and a charming love song called the "Duetto." The complete set has been recorded by Daniel Barenboim (two CDs; Deutsche Grammophon 423931-2 GGA2), selections on an 1823 piano have been recorded by Richard Burnett (Amon Ra SAR CD-38), and an interesting arrangement for guitar has been made by the English Guitar Quartet (Saydisc CD-SDL 379).

GUSTAV MAHLER

b. 1860, Kalischt, Bohemia (Czechoslovakia)
d. 1911, Vienna, Austria

Mahler was the Romantic era's most original symphonist, composing symphonies that were as large and stormy as the Romantic temperament. He was also the age's greatest conductor, a demanding taskmaster who raised the level of musicianship wherever he worked, even as he antagonized musicians who were little used to the demands he placed upon them.

Like Mendelssohn, Mahler was an outcast, a Jewish artist in a fiercely Protestant land. Unlike Mendelssohn, Mahler was not born to a financially secure or happy family. His father was a small-time innkeeper who beat his mother. The large family of ten siblings was stalked by tragedy: diphtheria took the lives of five of the children, one sister died of a brain tumor, a brother who was particularly close to young Gustav died of heart failure after a long and agonizing illness, and another brother, ashamed by his lack of talent, committed suicide. The entire family was affected by the hand of death; one sister would surround her bed with lighted candles and lie motionless for hours, imagining herself dead.

Mahler found his escape from the harsh realities of his family life when, at the age of six, he discovered a piano in his grandmother's attic. He took a single-minded interest in the instrument, teaching himself to play. His father had no ambitions for his son beyond the innkeeping trade, but, realizing that he had unusual musical capabilities, took him at age fifteen to the Vienna Conservatory of Music to see if he had the talent to support himself as a musician. The young Mahler played his own compositions for his audition, and the professor who heard him play was so impressed that he pronounced him a "born musician." And so Mahler escaped the fate of innkeeping to become a conservatory student.

From the conservatory, Mahler began his slow climb up the musical ladder. His first employment was as the conductor for a small-time music-hall orchestra. His first break came at age twenty-five, when he was invited to conduct a work by Mendelssohn in Leipzig. His performance was so impressive that he was immediately offered a job in Prague, and other employment followed in major cities.

Finally, at age thirty-seven he was invited to lead the Vienna Court Opera Orchestra. This post carried considerable prestige, even though the orchestra itself was in great disarray. The musicians were used to performing with little or no rehearsal, and the scores that they used were often truncated, poorly transcribed versions of the works. But Mahler was a perfectionist, and he established strict new rules for all of the musicians and the audience. Mahler would not allow latecomers to be seated once a performance began, he introduced new works to the repertory and tidied up the old standards, and he dismissed singers who were past their prime and musicians who failed to measure up to his standards.

Although everyone agreed that Mahler had greatly improved the orchestra, there was much grumbling within the musical community because of his high-handed attitude. There were also those who resented the fact that a poor Jewish man could have risen to such an important position. Mahler was able to hang onto his post for a decade through sheer determination; a lesser man would have resigned much sooner.

Meanwhile, Mahler began creating his great symphonic works. These large-scale pieces burst the notion of a "symphony" at the seams. The contemporary audience was not terribly sympathetic to these long and long-winded compositions. Mahler was unperturbed by the audience's reaction, secure in the notion that he was expanding musical horizons. He seemed to enjoy defying his audience, answering his critics with the cryptic words, "My time will come."

In 1907, Mahler gave up his post in Vienna to become director of the Metropolitan Opera Orchestra and the New York Philharmonic. His schedule became increasingly hectic with premieres in America and Europe. Mahler continued to be a demanding taskmaster, placing equally heavy demands on himself. In 1911, years of hard work finally took their toll: he collapsed in the early winter, suffering from a streptococcus infection. He asked to be returned to his native Vienna, where he lapsed into dementia. Waving his finger to direct an imaginary orchestra, he died with the name "Mozart" on his lips.

Recommended Listening

For those listeners who like their music to be "big," Mahler is the composer who can really fill the bill. He only composed symphonies, because only symphonies were big enough to capture his imagination. Although he wrote traditional symphonies of three movements, he often chose to go beyond these limits, pushing out to five or six parts, creating works that lasted twice as long as their traditional counterparts. Mahler engorged the orchestra with additional members, adding onto it mammoth choirs to achieve his desired effects. These works were so large in conception and demanded so many musicians that one of his later symphonies was nicknamed the "Symphony of a Thousand."

Although many of his works are bloated, Mahler achieved monumental effects, charting a personality of deep pessimism, torn by deep-seated conflicts. The emotional turmoil of Mahler's music strongly appealed to 20th-century audiences. Mahler's musical effects, such as restlessly shifting keys or purposely choosing dissonant harmonies, were influential on the expansion of musical expression in our time.

Only two of Mahler's symphonies are often revived today, the first and second. The first is one of two symphonies that Mahler composed with the standard number of movements, a traditional orchestra, and the usual running length. Nicknamed "The Titan," it was meant to portray the vast power of nature. Mahler underscored the programmatic nature of the work in a famous performance in 1894, when he arranged for cue cards to be held up before each part of the work describing the musical scene that was to be portrayed. In one section, titled "Human Comedy," Mahler has fashioned an ironic funeral march that echoes the children's round "Frère Jacques."

The second symphony, composed five years later, is more typical of Mahler's vision. It is scored for a large orchestra, including offstage horns and trumpets, unusual percussion instruments including sticks and gongs, and two vocal soloists and a chorus. The theme of this work is human life. Mahler named it "Redemption" and saw it as a reply to the unremitting darkness of his first symphony. Typical of Mahler, this is hardly a lighthearted celebration of human life. Instead, it is an unremitting questioning of the "whys" and "wherefores" of human existence, to give us a reason, in the composer's own words, "to continue living, yes, even if we are only to continue dying." The joyous climax comes only through the difficult suffering of the entire work. Although the work ends with an affirmation of human life, it is one that has been dearly paid for.

The first symphony is available in recordings by Maurice Abravanel and the Utah Symphony Orchestra (Vanguard Classics OVC 4003), Leonard Bernstein and the Royal Concertgebouw Orchestra (Deutsche Grammophon 423303-2 GH), and Sir Georg Solti and the London Symphony Orchestra (London 417701-2 LM). Zubin Mehta and the Israel Philharmonic have recorded the work with the addition of the second movement, originally a part of the symphony that was later dropped by the composer (Angel

CDC-49044). The second symphony has been recorded by the
Utah Symphony with Beverly Sills as one of the soloists (Vanguard Classics OVC 4003), as well as by Kiri Te Kanawa with the
Boston Symphony directed by Seiji Ozawa on a two-CD set (Philips
420824-2 PH2).

JOHANNES BRAHMS

b. 1833, Hamburg, Germany

d. 1897, Vienna, Austria

Although Brahms was born after many of the other Romantic
composers, he was the closest in spirit to Beethoven. He is often
called the most Classical of the Romantic composers and was
hailed in his day as Beethoven's spiritual heir. In temperament
and background, Brahms also shared many similarities with the
great German composer.

Born in intense poverty in one of the rougher neighborhoods of
Hamburg, Brahms had a difficult childhood. His father was a
second-rate musician and his mother a seamstress. The two fought
incessantly, making Brahms's home life unhappy at best. He did
poorly in school, where he found academic studies stultifying,
and his teachers often beat him when he failed to attend to his
work.

The one light in the young man's life was the piano. He quickly
showed ability on the instrument, composing his own melodies
and inventing a music-notation system so he could save his works.
His father hired a local piano teacher to aid in his studies. Brahms
gave his first recital at fourteen and was already working as a
honky-tonk pianist in the red-light district earning extra income
for his family. Under the pseudonyms of G. W. Marks and Karl
Wurth, among others, Brahms wrote simple piano pieces and
made simplified arrangements of well-known works for a local
music publisher.

Brahms's life changed in 1853 when he met the noted violinist
Eduard Reményi. This Hungarian virtuoso was touring Europe
and hired Brahms as his accompanist. Brahms immediately showed
his ability to meet the unusual demands of life on the road. In the
little town of Celle, the pianist discovered that his instrument was

out of tune by a half step. He quickly solved the problem, transcribing by sight all of his parts and playing them a half step higher.

Brahms's association with Reményi brought him into contact with many of the important musicians, composers, and patrons of the arts of the day. Franz Liszt asked to meet Brahms when the young pianist came to Weimar. Brahms, anxious to please but wary of Liszt's reputation as an excellent pianist, was too nervous to play for him. Instead, he gave him a copy of one of his compositions for Liszt to play. The elder composer was so impressed that he asked Brahms to critique one of his own compositions, only to discover the young man had fallen asleep during his performance of it! Brahms's unusual behavior did not dampen Liszt's enthusiasm for his work, and Liszt presented him with a cigarette case as a memento when he left town.

A stop in Düsseldorf brought Brahms into contact with two people who would become surrogate parents and musical inspirations to him: Robert and Clara Schumann. It took some coaxing to convince Robert to listen to him perform, but as soon as Brahms started to play, the elder composer leapt up and called his wife in from the kitchen, crying "Clara, you must come and hear music such as you've never heard before." Brahms was invited into the Schumann household, where he lived for three months. One month after meeting Brahms, Schumann enthusiastically singled him out in an important music-journal article, launching the young man's career.

Sadly, Brahms's friendship with Robert Schumann was short-lived. Schumann went insane, ending up in an asylum. Brahms returned to Düsseldorf to visit the composer, care for his children, and comfort his wife. Schumann died in 1856, leaving Brahms without a mentor. However, he remained close to Schumann's wife Clara for the next forty years, corresponding with her in great detail about his life's work. Although he deeply loved her, and respected her opinions of his music, he never married her or any other woman. Brahms was a misanthrope, comparing the difficulties of marriage to the difficulties of writing an opera (he never did either), disdainfully dismissing women as "fetters" that he could not bear.

Success did not come easily to the composer. His first chance to compose for orchestra came when he gained employment as music master to the Prince of Lippe-Detmold in 1857. He composed two serenades and a concerto for piano and orchestra that he premiered two years later in Hanover, playing the piano part himself with his old friend and advisor Joseph Joachim leading the orchestra. The performance was a failure, but Brahms was undismayed, vowing to work harder than ever. He spent the early 1860s in Hamburg and made his first trip to Vienna, where he was well received as a pianist even though his compositions were not terribly popular. His reception there was better than in his native Germany, though, so he settled in Vienna in the mid-1860s. By the early 1870s, his works were gaining greater acclaim.

In 1873, Brahms had his first unqualified success with the "Variations on a Theme by Haydn." This encouraged him to embark on a larger orchestral project, a symphony. All the while, he was conscious of the ghost of Beethoven hovering over him. He worked slowly, taking four years to make sketches, and finally completed the Symphony No. 1 in C Minor in 1876. Critics have called it the "tenth symphony," because in many ways it culminates and continues the traditions that Beethoven established in his nine symphonies. Brahms composed three other symphonies from 1877 to 1884.

By the early 1880s, Brahms was a celebrated and venerated figure in Viennese life, with many students, patrons, and followers. Still, his unusual character—much like the character of Beethoven—made him a figure of some amusement as well as veneration. He was sometimes warm and friendly to his students, and other times brusque and impatient. Although as an artist he was shrewd, organized, and ambitious, in his dress and housekeeping he was offhand and sloppy, wearing the same old clothes for many years and keeping a pile of manuscripts, correspondence, unpaid bills, and bundles of money in his rooms. Brahms was a sharp businessman, but tightfisted with money, always traveling third class and staying in inexpensive lodgings. When he died, he left an estate worth $100,000, an enormous sum for that time and an unbelievably large estate for a musician.

Although Brahms was viewed by some as hopelessly old-fashioned in his musical expression, he remained an active member of the Viennese musical community until his death in 1897. It is fitting that his death was caused by a fever that he caught while attending the funeral of his old love and patron, Clara Schumann. The Viennese press reported that Brahms's funeral attracted "prominent artists and celebrated men and women who came from afar to pay their last homage" to him.

Recommended Listening

Orchestral Works

Of Brahms's four symphonies, the first remains the best known and most often performed. In its marriage of deep emotions and highly developed classical form, it clearly shows the heritage of Beethoven. The other three bear listening, varying in mood from the sunny, idyllic nature of the second to the elegiac last symphony, with its unusual final movement in the form of a passacaglia, a dance preferred by the Classical composers but never before heard in a symphony.

The complete Brahms symphonies are available on a four-CD set by Leonard Bernstein and the Vienna Philharmonic (Deutsche Grammophon 415570-2 GX4) and by Herbert von Karajan and the Berlin Philharmonic on a three-CD set (Deutsche Grammophon 427602-2 GH3), which also includes the "Haydn Variations." A famous historic recording is Toscanini's version with the NBC Symphony; while not "hi-fi," few can match this legendary conductor's skills (RCA Gold Seal 60325-2 RG; four CDs). The first symphony is available alone in recordings by Bernstein (Deutsche Grammophon 4100881-2 GH), von Karajan (Deutsche Grammophon 423141-2 GHY), Sir Colin Davis with the Bavarian Radio Symphony Orchestra (RCA Red Seal 60382-2-RC), and by Zubin Mehta and the New York Philharmonic on a budget-priced CD (Odyssey YT-42486).

Brahms composed only one concerto for violin and orchestra, as a gift to Joseph Joachim. This 1876 work is quite demanding on the violinist; many passages are so hard to play that famous conductor Hans von Bülow made the oft-quoted remark that the piece is less a work for violin than against it! There are many recordings of this work available, including Isaac Stern with the Philadelphia Orchestra under the baton of Eugene Ormandy in a recording from the '60s (Sony Classical SBK 46335) that also includes Brahms's Concerto in A Minor for Violin, Cello, and Orchestra; Jascha Heifetz with the Chicago Symphony, a historic recording from the early '60s (RCA Red Seal RCD1-5402); and Yehudi Menuhin with the Lucerne Festival Orchestra (Angel CDH-63496), a historic recording made in 1949 that also includes the violin and cello concerto.

As a great pianist, Brahms was naturally attracted to composing for that instrument. He wrote two piano concerti, the first being the better known today, although it was poorly received when it was first performed. The audience that first heard it was put off by its gloomy, introspective nature. Composed in 1856 when the composer was twenty-three, it may have been inspired by the death of his mentor Schumann. The second concerto came later in the composer's career and reflects his greater command of the orchestra. This work lacks the emotionality of the first concerto but makes up for it in intellectual depth and quality of construction. The first concerto is available in recordings by Claudio Arrau with the Royal Concertgebouw Orchestra (Philips 4220702-2 PM), Daniel Barenboim with the New Philharmonia Orchestra (Angel CDM-63536), and Rudolf Serkin with the Cleveland Orchestra (Columbia Masterworks MK-42261). The second concerto can be heard performed by Vladimir Ashkenazy with the London Symphony conducted by Zubin Mehta (London 417710-2 LM) and by Vladimir Horowitz in a historic recording with Arturo Toscanini and the NBC Symphony recorded live in Carnegie Hall (RCA Gold Seal 60523-2-RG).

Chamber Works

Brahms wrote several chamber works for piano and strings, the best known being his Piano Quintet from 1862. This piece had a difficult birth, with the composer first scoring it for strings but, finding that unsatisfactory, he then scored it as a piano duet. Finally, he hit on the idea of piano with a string quartet, and the result is one of the great works of the classical canon. Like his earlier piano quartets, this has a youthful vitality and zestfulness.

Vladimir Ashkenazy has recorded it with the Cleveland Orchestra String Quartet (London 425839-2 LH), and Christoph Eschenbach with the Amadeus Quartet on a three-CD set that includes other chamber works by Brahms (Deutsche Grammophon 419875-2 GCM3).

Brahms's other noteworthy chamber work is the Clarinet Quintet that was composed in 1891 for clarinetist Richard Mühlfeld, one of the first masters of the instrument. As you might expect, this piece reflects the somber mood of old age, with a deep thoughtfulness that is the antithesis of the playful character of Brahms's earlier chamber works. The Berkshire String Quartet performs this work on Musicmasters 5027-2-C.

Solo Piano Works

Brahms wrote many piano pieces for his own performance and amusement. He wrote some "major" works, such as the variations on themes by Handel and Paganini, plus many other pieces in popular dance forms—such as waltzes and light capriccios (little caprices or whimsical pieces) and intermezzi. He also composed rhapsodies in the manner of Liszt, grand works expressing fiery Romantic emotions. Selections of Brahms's better-known piano works have been recorded by Emanuel Ax (Sony Classical SK-45933), Van Cliburn (RCA Red Seal 7942-2-RG), Vladimir Horowitz (RCA Gold Seal 60523-2-RG), and André Watts (Angel CDC 49094).

PIOTR ILYICH TCHAIKOVSKY

b. 1840, Votinsk, Russia

d. 1893, St. Petersburg, Russia

Tchaikovsky had perhaps the saddest life story of all of the Romantic composers. Plagued by periods of intense hypochondria and depression, a closet homosexual who could not acknowledge his sexual tendencies, Tchaikovsky was a hypersensitive, ill-adjusted man whose life ran to high peaks and distressingly low valleys. Despite this fact, and the fact that he did not embark on a musical career until his twenties, he was an amazingly prolific composer.

Tchaikovsky showed remarkable facility and interest in music from his early years. He was able to reproduce melodies on the piano from a single hearing at the age of five and once complained to his parents that musical melodies interrupted his sleep. Still, his parents chose a conservative career for the youngster, the law, and Tchaikovsky pursued legal studies through his early twenties.

In law school, Tchaikovsky was regarded as something of a gadabout and fop; uninterested in his studies, he rarely made the effort to compete, spending most of his spare time at the opera. By 1860, Tchaikovsky began surreptitiously studying music and composed some short works. In 1862, he decided to abandon the law and entered the St. Petersburg Conservatory. Writing to his sister, he said, "Whether I become a famous composer or a poor music teacher is a matter of indifference to me. At all events, my conscience will be clear and I shall no longer have the right to complain about my lot."

When he graduated from the conservatory in the mid-1860s, Tchaikovsky was desperate to make a living as a musician. The brother of one of his teachers was just then establishing a new music school in Moscow and offered the young composer a job at the outrageously low salary of five rubles a month. Still, it was better than nothing, and Tchaikovsky was surprised to find that his natural nervousness and hypochondria dissipated when he was teaching.

Tchaikovsky wrote his first symphony in this period, and it was premiered in 1868, followed by an opera and the famous *Romeo and Juliet* overture, the first mature work from the composer. He also conducted several unfortunate love affairs, finally wedding one of his music students whom he knew he didn't love. Tchaikovsky hoped through marriage to suppress what he called his "inclinations" or homosexual tendencies. The marriage was a catastrophe from day one; he could not bear to be alone with his wife, leading to his complete nervous breakdown.

At this same time, Tchaikovsky became acquainted with his most important patron, Nadezhda Filaretovna von Meck. They conducted a thirteen-year relationship, tinged with sexuality, but on strict terms imposed by the wealthy woman. She did not allow the composer to meet her; this suited him fine, because he was nervous around women. Their relationship was conducted entirely by mail, and the patron provided the composer with an annual stipend that enabled him to leave teaching and focus on composing.

It was in this period that Tchaikovsky enjoyed his greatest freedom. He traveled through Europe, composing many noteworthy works, including his fourth and fifth symphonies. His social and work habits became more normal, and he seemed to have overcome his earlier nervousness.

In 1890, his relationship with von Meck ended under mysterious circumstances. Although he was no longer financially dependent on her, the composer felt crushed emotionally. It is unclear why the stipend was withdrawn, although some have suggested that her family pressured her to end a relationship that was leading to rumor and innuendo. Others say she discovered the composer's homosexuality.

In 1891, Tchaikovsky came to America, where he was surprised to find that he was a venerated and well-known composer. He conducted his famous "Overture 1812" at the opening of Carnegie Hall, and the piece has remained a concert favorite. He loved the American spirit, although he felt he could not participate in the happiness of the new land. "I enjoy all this like a person sitting at a table set with marvels of gastronomy, devoid of appetite," he lamented.

On returning to Russia, his mood darkened. He composed his last symphony, the sixth or "Pathétique," during this period of emotional upheaval. He feared insanity, and the piece portrays the "dark night of the soul" in all of its gloomy terrors. Like many of Tchaikovsky's works, it was not well received on its premiere in 1893, although it has become one of the most-admired pieces in the Romantic symphonic repertoire.

In November of 1893, a cholera epidemic swept Moscow. Tchaikovsky foolishly drank a cup of unboiled water, exposing himself to the disease. Some say this was an intentional attempt to commit suicide. Whatever the case, he fell ill and soon died.

Recommended Listening

Orchestral Works

Tchaikovsky's fourth and sixth symphonies are most often performed today. They represent two sides of the composer's personality, one bright and sunny, the other dark and foreboding. The fourth symphony was written during the height of Tchaikovsky's epistolary friendship with his patron, von Meck. It is a kind of valentine to her, written in appreciation of the support she gave him both financially and emotionally. In uncharacteristic words, Tchaikovsky wrote von Meck that the last movement, and the symphony as a whole, depicted the simple pleasures of life. "If you find no pleasure in yourself," the composer said, "Look about you. Go to the people. . . . Rejoice in the happiness of others, and you will be able to live."

The Symphony No. 6 was named the "Pathétique" by Tchaikovsky's brother and confidant, Modeste. It depicts the darkness that haunted the composer. Written in his last year of life, it has sometimes been called "suicide music," because of the somber nature of the first and closing movements. There has never been a bleaker piece of music in the classical repertoire.

The six complete symphonies are available in a recording by Igor Markevitch and the London Symphony Orchestra on Philips 426848-2 PB4, a four-CD set. The fourth symphony is available in recordings from Claudio Abbado leading the Vienna Philharmonic Orchestra (Deutsche Grammophon 429527-2 GMF), along with the second symphony; Leonard Bernstein and the New York Philharmonic (Columbia Masterworks MYK-37766); and Eugene Ormandy and the Philadelphia Orchestra (Sony Classical SBK 46334), which also includes the famous "Overture 1812." The sixth symphony is available from Vladimir Ashkenazy and the Philharmonia Orchestra (London 411615-2 LH); von Karajan and the Berlin Philharmonic, along with the fourth and fifth symphonies (a three-CD set; Angel CDMC 69883); and Kurt Masur and the Leipzig Gewandhaus Orchestra (Teldec 43340 ZK).

Tchaikovsky wrote two well-known concerti, one for piano (Concerto No. 1 in B-flat) and the other for violin (Concerto in D Major). The piano concerto is famous for the beautiful folk theme that Tchaikovsky said he heard sung on the streets by a blind beggar. This melody was used for the schmaltzy hit of the '40s "Tonight We Love." The violin concerto is more Classical in nature, but it also features Romantic moments and hints of folk melodies. The piano concerto has been recorded many times, including a recording by Emil Gilels with Zubin Mehta conducting the New York Philharmonic Orchestra (Sony Classical SBK 46339), a recording that also includes the violin concerto. Van Cliburn recorded the piano concerto with the RCA Symphony (RCA 5912-2-RC), and Misha Dichter performed it with the Boston Symphony on a recording that also includes the violin concerto (RCA Papillon Collection 6526-2 RG).

Besides the symphonies, the best-known work by Tchaikovsky is the "Overture 1812." Like the works of Mahler, this features an expanded orchestra, featuring real cannons for the famous "battle scenes." The two opposing armies are represented by the national anthems of Russia and France ("God Save the Czar" versus "La Marseillaise"). The two themes duke it out, until finally the Russians emerge victorious. This is also the music that was used in the late '60s to sell Quaker Puffed Rice ("It is the cereal that's shot from guns!")

There are many recordings of this old chestnut, including Daniel Barenboim with the Chicago Symphony Orchestra (Deutsche Grammophon 400035-2 GH) and Mstislav Rostropovich and the National Symphony (Erato 45415-2 ZK), which also includes the fifth symphony.

Ballet Music

Tchaikovsky is famous for his scores for ballets, particularly *Swan Lake* and the perennial Christmas favorite *The Nutcracker*. The "Nutcracker Suite" is a famous selection of the best-loved dance melodies from the full ballet score and is available in many recordings. Arthur Fiedler and the Boston Pops recorded it on a CD entitled *Classics for Children* that also includes Sergei Prokofiev's "Peter and the Wolf" and Camille Saint-Saëns's "Carnival of the Animals" (RCA Gold Seal 6718-2 RG). Herbert von Karajan and the Berlin Philharmonic have a fine CD that includes *Swan Lake* and *Sleeping Beauty* as well as the "Nutcracker Suite" (Deutsche Grammophon 419175-2 GH).

Tchaikovsky Comes Out of the Closet

Many modern would-be Sigmund Freuds have analyzed Tchaikovsky's unhappy life as arising from his repressed homosexuality. It is interesting to note that his brother, Modeste, was an open homosexual, and it was only in letters to Modeste that Tchaikovsky was able to discuss his "inclinations," as he euphemistically called them.

Certainly Tchaikovsky was a fragile personality, highly dependent on the love and affection of others. It is unfortunate that he felt he had to deny his sexual feelings, as it undoubtedly contributed to his unhappiness. The letters to his brother chart his unhappy struggle to maintain his sanity and creativity. They mirror the famous correspondence of Vincent van Gogh and his brother, Theo, and make for fascinating reading for those interested in the history of music or of human mores.

RECORD COMPANY ADDRESSES

To help you find the recordings listed in this book, here are the addresses of all of the record labels mentioned. Some of the larger labels may not be willing to sell their CDs by mail order, but at least they can provide you with a catalog that you can use to order these recordings from other sources (mail-order catalogs or your friendly local record dealer). Happy hunting!

Allegretto. *See* Vox/Vox Unique/Turnabout.

Allegro Imports
3434 SE Milwaukie Avenue
Portland, OR 97202

Amon Ra. *See* Qualiton Imports.

Angel Records
1750 North Vine Street
Hollywood, CA 90028

Arabesque
60 East 42nd Street
New York, NY 10165

Arion. *See* Allegro Imports.

Astoria. *See* Allegro Imports.

Bellaphon. *See* Allegro Imports.

Bertelsman Music Group
1133 Avenue of the Americas
New York, NY 10036

BMG Classics. *See* Bertelsman Music Group.

Chandos. *See* Koch International.

Chrysalis. *See* Angel Records.

Claves. *See* Qualiton Imports.

Columbia Masterworks/Sony Classical
P.O. Box 4450
New York, NY 10101

Denon Records
135 West 50th Street, Suite 1915
New York, NY 10020

Deutsche Grammophon. *See* Polygram Classics.

Deutsche Harmonia Mundi. *See* Bertelsman Music Group.

Dorian Recordings
17 State Street, Suite 2E
Troy, NY 12180

ECM. *See* Polygram Classics.

Editio Classica. *See* Bertelsman Music Group.

Enigma Classics. *See* Angel Records.

Erato. *See* Nonesuch Records.

Ermitage. *See* Qualiton Imports.

ESS.A.Y.
145 Palisade Street, Suite 341
Dobbs Ferry, NY 10522

Europa Musica. *See* Koch International.

Fonè. *See* Allegro Imports.

Forlane. *See* Koch International.

Globe. *See* Qualiton Imports.

Green Linnet
43 Beaver Brook Road
Danbury, CT 06810

Harmonia Mundi USA
3364 South Robertson Boulevard
Los Angeles, CA 90034

Hungaroton. *See* Qualiton Imports.

Hyperion. *See* Harmonia Mundi USA.

Intercord. *See* Allegro Imports.

Intersound
Hembree Crest Center
11810 Wills Road
Roswell, GA 30077

Koch International
177 Cantiague Rock Road
Westbury, NY 11590

London. *See* Polygram Classics.

MCA Classics
70 Universal City Plaza
Universal City, CA 91608

Musicmasters
1710 Highway 35
Ocean, NJ 07712

Muza. *See* Koch International.

Nimbus
220 West 57th Street
New York, NY 10019

Nonesuch Records
75 Rockefeller Plaza
New York, NY 10019

Odyssey. *See* Columbia Masterworks/Sony Classical.

Oiseau/Oiseau-Lyre. *See* Polygram Classics.

Olympia. *See* Allegro Imports.

Paraclete Records
Box 1568
Hilltop Plaza, Route 6A
Orleans, MA 02653

Pavane. *See* Qualiton Imports.

Pearl. *See* Koch International.

Philips. *See* Polygram Classics.

Pierre Vernay. *See* Allegro Imports.

Polygram Classics
Worldwide Plaza
825 8th Avenue
New York, NY 10019

Preiser. *See* Koch International.

Pro Arte. *See* Intersound.

Qualiton Imports
24-02 40th Avenue
Long Island City, NY 11101

RCA Red Seal. *See* Bertelsman Music Group.

Saydisc. *See* Qualiton Imports.

Smithsonian Collection
One World Records
1250 West Northwest Highway, Suite 505
Palatine, IL 60067

Sony Classical. *See* Columbia Masterworks/Sony Classical.

Supraphonet. *See* Koch International.

Tactus. *See* Koch International.

Telarc Records
23307 Commerce Park Road
Beachwood, OH 44122

Teldec. *See* Nonesuch Records.

Titanic. *See* Harmonia Mundi USA.

Turnabout. *See* Vox/Vox Unique/Turnabout.

Vanguard Classics
Omega Record Group
15 West 72nd Street, Suite 35C
New York, NY 10022

Victoria. *See* Qualiton Imports.

Virgin Classics
30 West 21st Street
New York, NY 10010

Vox/Vox Unique/Turnabout
c/o Essex Entertainment
75 Essex Street
Hackensack, NJ 07601

Warner Brothers Records
3300 Warner Boulevard
Burbank, CA 91510

Wergo. *See* Harmonia Mundi USA.

White Label. *See* Qualiton Imports.

Timeline of Musical and World Events

Date	Musical Event	World Event
1600	Beginning of Baroque era; recorders introduced in England; Giles Farnaby (born c. 1563), British keyboardist, dies	
1603		Queen Elizabeth I of England dies; James I rules through 1625
1605		Guy Fawkes tries to blow up the British Parliament
1607	*Orfeo* (opera) by Monteverdi premiered	

Date	Musical Event	World Event
1610		Louis XIII takes throne in France (rules through 1643)
1616		William Shakespeare dies
1619	*The Fitzwilliam Virginal Book* published (collection of English keyboard music)	William Harvey, English anatomist, discovers the circulation of the blood
1621	Jan Pieterszoon Sweelinck (b. 1562), Dutch organist, dies	
1623	William Byrd (b. 1543), British composer, dies	
1628	John Bull (b. 1562), British organist, dies	
1629		Charles I dissolves Parliament
1632	Jean-Baptiste Lully, French composer, born (d. 1687)	
1635		Peace of Prague signed between Emperor Ferdinand II and the Elector of Saxony
1637	Dietrich Buxtehude, German organist, born (d. 1707)	
1639	*Adone* (opera) by Monteverdi premiered	
1642		English Civil War (through 1650)

Date	Musical Event	World Event
1643	Girolamo Frescobaldi (b. 1583), Italian organist, dies	Louis XIV crowned in France (rules through 1715)
1649		Charles I of England beheaded
1653	Arcangelo Corelli, Italian violinist and composer, born (d. 1713); Johann Pachelbel born (d. 1706)	Oliver Cromwell made Lord Protector of England (rules through 1658)
1657		Leopold I made Holy Roman Emperor (rules through 1705)
1659	Henry Purcell, British composer, born (d. 1695); Alessandro Scarlatti, Italian opera composer and father of Domenico, born (d. 1725)	
1660		Charles II returns to England, takes throne in 1661
1666	First known Stradivarius violin made	
1668	François Couperin, French keyboardist and composer, born (d. 1733); Dietrich Buxtehude becomes organist at Lübeck	
1675	Antonio Vivaldi, Italian violinist/composer, born (d. 1741)	

Date	Musical Event	World Event
1685	Johann Sebastian Bach, German organist/composer, born (d. 1750); George Frideric Handel, German composer, born (d. 1759); Domenico Scarlatti, Italian keyboardist/composer, born (d. 1757)	James II, King of England (through 1688) takes throne
1687	Francesco Geminiani, Italian violinist, born (d. 1762)	
1689		William and Mary become rulers of England; Peter the Great crowned Czar of Russia
1692	Giuseppe Tartini, Italian violinist/composer, born (d. 1770)	
1703	Antonio Vivaldi ordained as a priest	
1705		Joseph I made Holy Roman Emperor (rules through 1711)
1706		Benjamin Franklin born
1708	J. S. Bach employed as church organist at Weimar	
1709	Bartolommeo Cristofori (1665–1731), Italian instrument builder, makes first "pianofortes"	"Eau-de-cologne" (first man-made perfume) introduced in Cologne, Germany

Date	Musical Event	World Event
1710	Handel appointed ka-pellmeister to Elector George of Hanover (later King George I of England)	
1711	Tuning fork invented by John Shore (1662–1752), English trumpeter	Alexander Pope publishes his "Essay on Criticism"
1713		Peace of Utrecht; Frederick William I made King of Prussia
1714	Carl Philip Emmanuel Bach born (d. 1788)	George I, King of England (through 1727)
1715		Louis XV, King of France (through 1774)
1716	*L'art de toucher le clavecin* published by F. Couperin	
1717	Handel's "Water Music" performed for the first time; F. Couperin appointed harpsichord-ist to the French King, J. S. Bach made orchestral director in Cöthen	Inoculation for smallpox introduced in England
1719	Leopold Mozart, violin-ist and father of Wolfgang Amadeus, born (d. 1787)	
1721	J. S. Bach composes Brandenburg Concerti	Peter the Great made Czar of Russia

Date	Musical Event	World Event
1722	J. S. Bach composes "The Well-tempered Clavier," Book 1	
1723	J. S. Bach becomes cantor at St. Thomas-schule in Leipzig	
1727		George II, King of England (through 1760)
1732	Franz Joseph Haydn, German composer, born (d. 1809)	George Washington born
1742	Handel's "Messiah" premieres	
1743		Thomas Jefferson born
1745	Johann Stamitz (1717–1757) takes over the Mannheim orchestra, making it the most famous orchestral ensemble of its day	
1746		Battle of Culloden, in which British wipe out the Scots
1749	"Royal Fireworks Music" by Handel performed	
1750	Baroque era ends; Classical period begins; Antonio Salieri, Italian composer and nemesis of Mozart, born (d. 1825)	Original Westminster Bridge constructed in England

Date	Musical Event	World Event
1751	The *Art of Playing the Violin*, first violin instruction book in English, written by Francesco Geminiani	
1752	Muzio Clementi, Italian pianist, born (d. 1832)	
1756	Wolfgang Amadeus Mozart born (d. 1791); father Leopold publishes his violin instruction book, *Violinschule*	First chocolate factory opens in Germany
1759	Haydn's first symphony premiered	Robert Burns, Scottish poet, born
1761	Haydn hired by Prince Paul Esterházy as chief musician for his estate	
1762	Benjamin Franklin perfects the glass harmonica	Catherine II of Russia takes the throne (rules through 1796)
1763		Peace of Paris ends Seven Years' War
1764	Mozart writes his first symphony (at age eight)	
1765		The Stamp Act passed by British Parliament
1766		Mason-Dixon Line drawn
1770	Mozart knighted by the Pope; Ludwig van Beethoven born (d. 1827)	Boston Massacre
1773		Boston Tea Party

Date	Musical Event	World Event
1774		Louis XVI takes French throne
1775–1783		American Revolution
1776	"Haffner" symphony of Mozart premiered	American Declaration of Independence
1778	Beethoven's first public performance (at age eight)	
1781	Mozart meets Haydn	
1782	Niccolò Paganini, Italian virtuoso violinist, born (d. 1840)	James Watt invents the steam engine
1783		Peace of Versailles signed
1787		U.S. Constitution ratified
1788	"Jupiter" symphony by Mozart premiered	
1789		George Washington elected first president of the U.S.; storming of the Bastille begins the French Revolution
1791	"Surprise" symphony by Haydn premiered; *The Magic Flute* by Mozart has its first performance	Bill of Rights ratified
1792	Haydn accepts Beethoven as his pupil	

Date	Musical Event	World Event
1795	Haydn's twelve "London" symphonies are performed	John Keats, British poet, born
1797	Franz Schubert, German composer, born (d. 1828)	Napoleon takes Paris
1799	Beethoven's first symphony composed	
1802		Napoleon takes Italy, declares himself King in 1805
1803	"Kreutzer" sonata composed by Beethoven	Louisiana Purchase
1804	"Eroica" symphony written by Beethoven	Nathaniel Hawthorne, American author, born
1808	Beethoven's fifth and sixth symphonies premiered	
1809	Felix Mendelssohn born (d. 1847)	Abraham Lincoln born
1810	Robert Schumann, German composer/music critic, born (d. 1856); Frédéric Chopin, Polish composer/pianist, born (d. 1849)	
1811	Franz Liszt, Hungarian pianist/composer, born (d. 1886)	

Date	Musical Event	World Event
1812		Napoleon invades Russia; U.S. declares war on England
1813	Giuseppe Verdi, Italian opera composer, born (d. 1901); Richard Wagner, German opera composer, born (d. 1883)	
1814	J. N. Maelzel invents the metronome in Vienna	Napoleon defeated and banished to Elba; Louis XVIII takes throne in France; Treaty of Ghent ends U.S./British conflict
1815		Battle of Waterloo: Wellington defeats Napoleon after his brief return to power
1818		Border between U.S. and Canada established on 49th parallel
1820	Classical period ends; Romantic period begins	King George IV takes throne in England (rules through 1830)
1822	"Unfinished" symphony by Schubert composed; Liszt makes his concert debut at age eleven	
1824	Beethoven's ninth symphony premiered	

Date	Musical Event	World Event
1825	Johann Strauss, German composer who popularized the waltz, born (d. 1899); Mendelssohn composes his overture to *A Midsummer Night's Dream*	Czar Nicholas takes throne in Russia
1829	Mendelssohn initiates a J. S. Bach revival with his performance of the "St. Matthew Passion"	
1830	Chopin leaves his homeland, Poland, for good	William IV becomes King of England
1833	Johannes Brahms, German composer, born (d. 1897)	
1836		Davy Crockett killed at the Alamo
1837		Queen Victoria takes the throne of England
1838	Chopin meets George Sand and begins his stormy love affair with her; Schubert's ninth symphony discovered in a trunk by Robert Schumann	
1840	Boehm fingering system comes into general use on the flute; Piotr Ilyich Tchaikovsky, Russian composer, born (d. 1893)	Pierre Renoir and Auguste Rodin, French artists, born

Date	Musical Event	World Event
1841	Antonin Dvořák, Czech nationalist composer, born (d. 1904); saxophone invented (patented in 1846)	
1842	New York and Vienna Philharmonic orchestras established; Boehm fingering system adopted for the clarinet; Mendelssohn's "Scotch" symphony premiered	
1843	Edvard Grieg, Norwegian nationalist composer, born (d. 1907); Mendelssohn's complete score for *A Midsummer Night's Dream* is performed	William Wordsworth appointed Poet Laureate of England
1851	Liszt composes his first Hungarian rhapsody	
1852		New French constitution makes Louis Napoleon Emperor (rules through 1870)
1853	Henry Steinway makes his first pianos in New York City; Brahms hired to accompany violinist Eduard Reményi	
1854	Schumann hospitalized for insanity; dies two years later	

Date	Musical Event	World Event
1855		Alexander II becomes Czar of Russia
1856		India made a British colony
1860	Gustav Mahler, German composer/ conductor, born (d. 1911)	Lincoln elected President of the U.S.
1861		U.S. Civil War begins (through 1865)
1862	Tchaikovsky drops out of law school to pursue the life of a musician; Brahms composes his piano quintet	Bismarck named Prime Minister of Prussia
1865	Edvard Grieg organizes first concert devoted to Norwegian composers; Schubert's "Unfinished" symphony has its first public performance	Lincoln assassinated
1869	Grieg meets Liszt, who becomes one of his most important defenders	Suez Canal opens
1870		Vladimir Lenin born
1873	"Variations on a Theme by Haydn," first work of Brahms to receive critical acclaim, premiered	

Date	Musical Event	World Event
1874	Brahms publishes his "Hungarian Dances"	Disraeli becomes Prime Minister of England (through 1880)
1875	Tchaikovsky's Piano Concerto No. 1 composed	
1876	Brahms's first symphony premiered; Pablo Casals, cellist/ conductor, is born (d. 1973); Grieg composes music for Ibsen's *Peer Gynt*	
1882	Igor Stravinsky, Russian modern composer, born (d. 1971); "Overture 1812" by Tchaikovsky premiered; Berlin Philharmonic founded	Franklin Delano Roosevelt born
1883	Original Metropolitan Opera House in New York City opens	
1885	Dvořák hired to teach at the National Conservatory of Music in New York City	Grover Cleveland inaugurated as 22nd U.S. president
1889		Adolph Hitler born
1891	Tchaikovsky conducts his "Overture 1812" at the opening of New York's Carnegie Hall	
1892	*The Nutcracker,* by Tchaikovsky, has its first performance	Diesel patents his internal combustion engine

Date	Musical Event	World Event
1893	Symphony "From the New World" by Dvořák has its premiere in New York; "Pathétique" symphony by Tchaikovsky composed	
1894	Mahler's first symphony performed	Nicholas II becomes Czar of Russia (through 1917, when he is executed by the Bolsheviks)
1895	Dvořák composes his "Humoresques"	
1896	Clara Schumann dies; "Also Sprach Zarathustra" by Richard Strauss has its first performance	
1898		Dreyfus affair in France; Spanish-American War
1900	Aaron Copland, American composer, born (d. 1990)	

GLOSSARY

Arpeggio. Playing the notes of a chord one after another rather than at the same time. *See also* Chord; Figured bass.

Baroque. Highly ornamented style of music born in Italy in the 17th century. The great Baroque composers include Vivaldi and Corelli.

Canon. A composition in which a group of vocalists or instrumentalists play the same melody, but each begins at a different time. Also called a round or catch.

Capriccio. A whimsical, short piano work.

Chaconne. A Baroque musical form that consists of one long variation on a melody. Closely related to the passacaglia.

Chorale. A Protestant hymn. In the chorale fantasia, a hymn tune is used as a basis for an organ fantasy or series of variations.

Chord. A grouping of three or more notes played simultaneously.

Clarinet. An endblown, single-reed instrument with a mellow tone, perfected in the 18th and 19th centuries.

Classical. A type of music that emphasizes the formal structure of a composition and the perfect balancing of each of its component parts.

Clavichord. An early keyboard instrument that produces tones through the action of tangents (or small metal hammers) that strike the strings from underneath.

Concertino. In the concerto grosso, the smaller part of the orchestra, usually consisting of two solo violins and cello with harpsichord accompaniment.

Concerto. A form of composition that features a solo instrument and orchestra, performing equally balanced but separate parts.

Concerto grosso. A development of the concerto by Arcangelo Corelli (1653–1713) and his contemporaries in which the orchestra is divided into two parts, the concertino and the ripieno.

Counterpoint. Literally, "point against point." Any composition in which two or more melodies are played simultaneously. *See also* Canon; Fugue.

Damper. In pianos and harpsichords, the mechanism that serves to stop or dampen the vibration of the strings after the key is released.

Divertissement. A collection of melodies loosely connected to form a longer work.

Equal temperament. The tuning system, sometimes called "just temperament," that allows for the equal spacing of the notes of the scale. Bach championed this tuning system in "The Well-tempered Clavier."

Escapement. The mechanism in the piano that allows the hammer to drop after striking the strings, so that the note may sound fully.

Étude. Literally, "study." In piano literature, an étude is a piece written to explore certain capabilities of the instrument.

Fantasia. An extended improvisation on, or elaboration of, a melody.

Figured bass. In early orchestral works, the harpsichord or other keyboard instrument was used as an accompaniment to the group. These accompanying "figured bass" parts were indicated in the scores through numbers, indicating the proper harmonies to be played (usually as arpeggios).

Flute. A wind instrument that is held transversely. Modern flutes (developed in the 19th century) feature the Boehm fingering system, a system of keys and levers that enables the instrument to play in tune while still allowing the player to finger it comfortably.

Form. The underlying structure of a musical composition.

Fugue. A form of counterpoint in which a subject or melody is introduced by one voice and then imitated by one or more other voices. The exposition consists of the statement of the subject through all of the voices. This is usually followed by an episode, often in a different key and featuring a new melody.

Fundamental (tone). The basic tone produced by a vibrating string or column of air. Partials or overtones are the higher-frequency tones produced by the divisions of the fundamental vibration into smaller vibrating sections. These partials are heard more softly (if at all) than the fundamental tone.

Harpsichord. A keyboard instrument that features plectra or picks that pluck the strings from below. The strings run at a 90-degree angle to the keyboard. Often, two keyboards (or manuals) are featured.

Homophony. A single melody line accompanied by a simple harmony part, often consisting of chords.

Impromptu. A brief piano composition favored by the Romantic composers, particularly Schubert. It is meant to have a casually put together feeling, as if the player were improvising.

Madrigal. A song sung by several voices in harmony. Madrigals were written on secular subjects, often based on classical mythology.

Mazurka. A moderately paced Polish folk dance in waltz time, although the accent falls on the third beat (rather than the first, as in the waltz). Popularized in classical music by Liszt.

Minuet. A stately dance form originally popularized in the 17th-century French court. Featured in the suite, the form remained popular into the age of symphonies, when many composers used it to replace the third movement of a symphony.

Mode. A group of scales discovered by the ancient Greeks and revived in the Middle Ages. Each mode is defined by the intervals between the notes, not by the starting tone as in a modern scale.

Modulation. To change from one key to another.

Movement. A section of a composition, such as a symphony.

Nocturne. Literally, "nightfall." A sad, wistful composition introduced by Irish composer John Field and popularized by Chopin.

Oboe. Double-reed wind instrument with a characteristic nasal sound.

Orchestra. A large group of instruments playing together. The modern orchestra is divided into four sections: strings, woodwinds, brass, and percussion.

Organ. A keyboard instrument featuring pipes that are mounted on a wind chamber. The keys control valves that open into the pipes, thus allowing them to sound.

Overture. An extended composition, originally played before a theatrical performance or before a suite. Eventually, overtures were played on their own and led to the development of the symphony.

Partita. *See* Suite.

Passacaglia. *See* Chaconne.

Pedalboard. The foot-activated keyboard on the organ that controls the bass notes.

Pianoforte. A keyboard instrument developed in 18th-century Italy and perfected over the next 150 years. The piano had an advantage over earlier keyboard instruments in that the player could control the dynamics (how loudly or softly the notes sounded). Tones are produced by hammers striking the strings from below.

Polonaise. Stately Polish folk dance, popularized by Liszt.

Polyphony. More than one melodic part played at the same time. *See also* Canon; Counterpoint; Fugue.

Prelude. Originally, the opening movement to a fugue or suite. Chopin and the Romantics used the term more loosely to describe a short piano composition.

Program music. Music that describes an external text or theme, such as Vivaldi's "The Four Seasons" or Tchaikovsky's "Overture 1812." *See also* Tone poem.

Recapitulation. The repetition of the principal theme of a composition, usually at the end of a movement or end of the piece.

Rhapsody. Liszt's adaptation of a traditional Hungarian dance form noted for its abrupt changes in rhythm and volume.

Ripieno. The entire orchestra (in the concerto grosso).

Romantic. A movement in the arts away from external form and structure to personal feeling and emotion.

Scale. Scales are defined by the pitch or note with which they begin (a "C scale" always begins with "C," etc.). There are two types of scales: major and minor.

Serenade. Literally "evening music," a piece written for a small orchestral ensemble to be performed in the open air.

Sonata. A piano work or a work for a solo instrument with piano accompaniment, often in four parts.

Sonata form. Refers to the form of each movement of a sonata (and also used in string quartets or symphonies). The form consists of two contrasting themes played in the following order: theme (A), countertheme (B), theme (A).

String quartet. A composition for two violins, viola, and cello.

Suite. A grouping of dance forms in order to create a longer composition, played by either a single instrument or a group. Also called a "partita."

Symphony. An extended composition for a large group of instruments or orchestra. Usually, the symphony has four movements, and each movement is written in the sonata form.

Theme and variation. A form of composition in which a melody is stated and then put through a series of variations in melody line, key, or rhythm.

Toccata. Literally, "touching." A free-form keyboard work characterized by rapid melodies and full chords.

Tone poem. An orchestral work inspired by either a literary work, a feeling, or a place. Also called a "symphonic poem."

Tremolo. The reaction of a twelve-year-old to watching *A Nightmare on Elm Street*. Also, the vibrating or trembling sound of a string (as on a violin) or vocalist, used to express deep emotion.

Trumpet. In Baroque times, a simple horn that played a single tone and its partials. Later, through the addition of valves and keys, a chromatic brass instrument.

Violin. A bowed, stringed instrument that is the lead voice in the string quartet and orchestra.

Waltz. An Austrian folk dance in 3/4 time, with the accent on the first beat, popularized around the turn of the 19th century.

BIBLIOGRAPHY

Anderson, David. *The Piano Makers.* New York: Pantheon Books, 1982.

Arnold, Denis. *The New Grove Italian and Baroque Masters.* New York: W. W. Norton, 1984.

Baines, Anthony. *Woodwind Instruments and Their History.* Rev. ed. New York: W. W. Norton, 1962.

Bernstein, Leonard. *The Joy of Music.* New York: Simon and Schuster, 1981.

Brown, Maurice J., and Eric Sams. *The New Grove Schubert.* New York: W. W. Norton, 1983.

Carlin, Richard. *The World of Music: European Classical Music, 1600–1825.* New York: Facts on File, 1988.

Cohn, Arthur. *Recorded Classical Music: A Critical Guide to Composers and Performances.* New York: Schirmer Books, 1981.

Copland, Aaron. *What to Listen for in Music.* Rev. ed. New York: Mentor Books, 1954.

Cross, Milton, and David Ewen. *Milton Cross' Encyclopedia of the Great Composers and Their Music.* New rev. ed. Garden City, NY: Doubleday, 1962.

Dean, Winton, and Anthony Hicks. *The New Grove Handel.* New York: W. W. Norton, 1983.

Downes, Edward. *The New York Philharmonic Guide to the Symphony*. New York: Walker, 1976.

Einstein, Alfred. *Music in the Romantic Era*. New York: W. W. Norton, 1947.

Ewen, David. *The Complete Book of Classical Music*. Englewood Cliffs, NJ: Prentice-Hall, 1965.

Gaines, James R. *The Lives of the Piano*. New York: Holt, Rinehart, and Winston, 1981.

Greenfield, Edward, ed. *The New Penguin Guide to Compact Discs and Cassettes*. New York: Penguin Books, 1988.

Haas, Kari. *Inside Music: How to Understand, Listen to, and Enjoy Good Music*. Garden City, NY: Doubleday, 1984.

Hemming, Roy. *Discovering Great Music: A New Listener's Guide to the Top Classical Composers and Their Masterworks on CDs, LPs, and Tapes*. New York: Newmarket Press, 1990.

Hindley, Geoffrey. *The Larousse Encyclopedia of Music*. New York: Crescent Books, 1989.

Hogwood, Christopher. *Handel*. New York: Thames and Hudson, 1985.

Keiman, Joseph, and Alan Tyson. *The New Grove Beethoven*. New York: W. W. Norton, 1983.

Kennedy, Michael. *Mahler*. 2nd ed. New York: Schirmer Books, 1991.

Kupferberg, Herbert. *Basically Bach*. New York: McGraw-Hill, 1985.

Landon, H. C. *Haydn*. New York: Praeger, 1972.

———*Mozart and Vienna*. New York: Schirmer Books, 1991.

———*The Mozart Compendium*. New York: Schirmer Books, 1991.

Larsen, Jens P., and Georg Feder. *The New Grove Haydn*. New York: W. W. Norton, 1983.

Loesser, Arthur. *Men, Women, and Pianos*. New York: Simon and Schuster, 1954.

Orlova, Alexandra. *Tchaikovsky: A Self-Portrait*. New York: Oxford University Press, 1990.

Palesca, Claude V. *Baroque Music*. Englewood Cliffs, NJ: Prentice-Hall, 1968.

Rosen, Charles. *The Classical Style: Haydn, Mozart, Beethoven.* New York: Viking, 1971.

Sadie, Stanley. *The New Grove Mozart.* New York: W. W. Norton, 1983.

Scholes, Percy. *The Oxford Companion to Music.* 9th ed. New York: Oxford University Press, 1958.

Schwarz, Boris. *Great Masters of the Violin.* New York: Simon and Schuster, 1983.

Skvorecky, Josef. *Dvořák in Love.* New York: W. W. Norton, 1988.

Soloman, Joseph. *Mozartiana: Two Centuries of Notes, Quotes, and Anecdotes about Wolfgang Amadeus Mozart.* New York: Random House, 1990.

Solomon, Maynard. *Beethoven.* New York: Schirmer Books, 1977.

Svejda, Jim. *The Record Shelf Guide to the Classical Repertoire.* 2nd ed. Rocklin, CA: Prima Publishing, 1990.

Taubman, Howard. *The New York Times Guide to Listening Pleasure.* New York: Macmillan, 1988.

Temperley, Nicholas, et al. *The New Grove Early Romantic Masters, I: Chopin, Schumann, and Liszt.* New York: W. W. Norton, 1985.

Todd, R. Larry. *Mendelssohn and His World.* Princeton, NJ: Princeton University Press, 1991.

Walker, Alan. *The Chopin Companion: Profiles of the Man and the Musician.* New York: W. W. Norton, 1973.

Wolff, Christoph, et al. *The New Grove Bach Families.* New York: W. W. Norton, 1983.

INDEX

About the Author

Richard Carlin is a long-time contributor to the Musical Heritage Society *Review*. He is the author of the five-volume *World of Music* series published by Facts on File, as well as other books, articles, and reviews on music instrumentation and history, and liner notes for numerous classical albums. He has produced ten albums of traditional Irish and American music for Folkways Records, and performs traditional dance music on the English concertina.